CONNECTING WITH CUSTOMERS

How to Sell, Service, and Market the Travel Product

Marc Mancini, Ph. D.

Department of Travel
West Los Angeles College

Prentice
Hall

Upper Saddle River, New Jersey 07458

Library of Congress Cataloging-in-Publication Data

Mancini, Marc, 1946–
   Connecting with customers : how to sell, service, and market the travel product / Marc Mancini.
     p. cm.
   Includes bibliographical references (p.)
   ISBN 0-13-093390-2
   1. Tourism—Marketing. 2. Travel agents. I. Title.

G155.A1 M2629 2003
338.4'791'0688—dc21

2002011542

Editor-in-Chief: Stephen Helba
Executive Editor: Vernon R. Anthony
Executive Assistant: Nancy Kesterson
Editorial Assistant: Ann Brunner
Associate Editor: Marion Gottlieb
Director of Manufacturing and Production: Bruce Johnson
Managing Editor: Mary Carnis
Senior Production Editor: Adele M. Kupchik
Marketing Manager: Ryan DeGrote
Production Management: Pine Tree Composition, Inc.
Production Editor: Russell Jones
Manufacturing Manager: Ilene Sanford
Manufacturing Buyer: Cathleen Petersen
Creative Director: Cheryl Asherman
Cover Design Coordinator: Christopher Weigand
Interior Design: Pine Tree Composition, Inc.
Printer/Binder: Banta Book Group
Cover Designer: Kevin Kall
Cover Printer: Phoenix Color

Pearson Education LTD
Pearson Education Australia PTY, Limited
Pearson Education Singapore, Pte. Ltd
Pearson Education North Asia Ltd
Pearson Education Canada, Ltd
Pearson Educación de Mexico, S.A. de C.V.
Pearson Education—Japan
Pearson Education Malaysia, Pte. Ltd

10 9 8 7 6 5 4 3 2 1

ISBN 0-13-093390-2

Contents

Preface

Is travel something very special to you? Do you enjoy the thought of helping other people have great vacations, too? Also, if you're already a travel professional, are you looking for ways to perform at an even higher level?

If your answer to any of these questions is *yes*, then *Connecting with Customers: How to Sell, Service, and Market the Travel Product* will provide interesting reading indeed. This book will help you explore the best ways to satisfy the travel needs of today's consumers. You'll uncover the marketing strategies that underlie selling and buying travel today. And you'll discover how to not just satisfy travel customers, but *delight* them. Even better: This voyage of learning, we hope, will be entertaining, too.

Many other travel sales and marketing books are out there. How is this one different?

- It applies sales, service, and marketing principles to *all* sectors of the industry: airlines, travel agencies, cruises, tours, lodging, car rentals, attractions, tourist bureaus, and more. The result: You can apply your knowledge to any travel situation.
- It takes the experiences you're familiar with from other sales and service industries and carefully *compares* them to what goes on in travel. By connecting the two, you'll understand travel-related selling and buying much more quickly. Moreover, you'll come to comprehend more fully the overall principles of sales, service, and marketing. This information will help you in all sectors of the business. It'll even help you become a better-informed consumer.
- It examines not just front-line sales, but *business-to-business* and *internal* sales, as well. That way you can apply your insights to all sorts of scenarios.
- It's thoroughly *up-to-date*. It examines today's e-environment of sales and service, *and* predicts where it's all going.
- It uses *lively* and *entertaining* prose to make your reading easily understood and fun.

- It provides *useful* and *practical solutions* for travel situations. Sure, you'll encounter theoretical explanations, but only to deepen your understanding of *why* certain things work and others don't.
- It deploys *an arsenal of tactics* to help you learn. Bullet points, objectives, a glossary, lists, charts, bold or italicized items, and sidebars organize this book's content so that you'll understand easily and remember more.
- Perhaps this textbook's most unique feature: It's *interactive.* Little activities throughout the text and major ones at each chapter's end will challenge you to apply, explore, and benefit from your new-found knowledge in ways that will make this book's message a *part of you.* In a sense, you will be this book's co-author!

HOW SHOULD YOU STUDY FROM THIS BOOK?

1. **Read with pen in hand.** *Connecting with Customers* is as much a workbook as it is a textbook. Complete those activities, answer those questions. Doing this will engage you in the material and fire up your insights. And don't worry about "ruining" your book. You're personalizing it to your experiences and with your thoughts.
2. **Pay special attention to bold or italicized concepts and words.** These are things you must know to succeed in travel. Reinforce additional key points by using different color highlighters.
3. **If any word or term is unclear to you, find out its meaning.** We've tried to limit this book's vocabulary to concepts that are familiar to people who know at least a little about travel. In many cases—just to be safe—industry terms are defined for you in the text, in the glossary, or both. A good dictionary (including the travel dictionaries listed in the bibliography) should clarify any terms we've overlooked.

"I WISH I'D KEPT THAT BOOK!"

You'd be surprised how often people say that. This textbook is an investment in your future. It has strategies that will come in handy later on, that you'll wish to refer to—even if you work in an entirely different business. And, after all, once you fill out the exercises, you will have helped write it!

TO THE INSTRUCTOR

We're delighted you've adopted *Connecting with Customers* for your students. You'll find that it provides a refreshing and rewarding approach to teaching three very critical subjects.

Connecting with Customers takes an ecumenical approach—all industry segments and situations are covered. No matter what travel career your students eventually pursue, they'll be prepared. This book also approaches its topics in the order that your students are likely to experience them: Sales and service first, marketing and more advanced topics later. Yes, its emphasis is on sales, but again, this is probably what your students will need to understand—especially today—in the early phase of their careers in travel. By alluding to other buying experiences, it permits your students—even those who've done little traveling—to relate to the content more quickly.

Connecting with Customers can serve as a stand-alone textbook or as a supplement to courses on virtually any facet of the travel industry (including introductory ones). It's appropriate to all instructional levels: Four-year colleges, two-year colleges, proprietary schools, and high schools. Most importantly, its unique, interactive format will support you in your efforts to involve your students—both in and outside the classroom—in a powerfully motivating way.

Connecting with Customers is supplemented by an Instructor's Manual that includes a test bank, thematic outlines, suggested answers to all activities and questions, and teaching tips that will help you connect to *your* customers: those future travel professionals.

ACKNOWLEDGMENTS

My sincerest thanks to Karen Fukushima, who assisted me in countless ways in this book's development, and to Rick Scarry, who created much of the book's supplementary work. My gratitude to the book's reviewers, Liping A. Cai, Purdue University; Catherine Melcher, Carlson Wagonlit Travel; and Stuart Schulman, Kingsborough Community College—The City University of New York, whose suggestions have been critical to tailoring *Connecting with Customers* to its market.

Marc Mancini
West Los Angeles

1
The Basics

OBJECTIVES

After reading this chapter, you'll be able to:

- Explain what sales, service, and marketing are

- Distinguish among the four different kinds of selling

- Identify the six essential steps of the sales cycle

- Explain why people buy travel

- Differentiate between commodities and experiences, perishable and nonperishable products, and transactional vs. consultative selling

Hawaii. Paris. A luxury cruise. A Caribbean resort.

How did reading those words make you feel? Almost surely the emotions you felt were warm, wonderful ones.

And that's why selling, serving, and marketing travel are such gratifying experiences. You're delivering happiness and fulfillment, enrichment and dreams. Very few salespeople, servicepeople, or marketing specialists in other industries can say that.

But before going any further, let's explore what selling, service, and marketing are all about. Only then can we really understand how travel fits into the big picture and discover what makes it a profoundly unique business.

Tropical beaches bring warm thoughts to most people's minds. *(Photo by Justus Ghormley)*

BUYING AND SELLING: AN OVERVIEW

Have you bought anything this week? The fact is, you've probably bought many things. Just to make sure, though, let's do a little exercise. In the space below, try to list every single thing you've bought in the last seven days:

Not easy, is it? The reason: We purchase so many things that buying becomes a seamless part of our everyday lives. It's hard to separate all those buying moments from everything else. Moreover, as you created the above list, you may have worried about what the word *thing* meant. Did it have to be a physical thing, like a cell phone? Or could it be something nonphysical, like insurance, stocks, a cable TV subscription or—yes—a vacation?

How about that word *buy*? Does it require the exchange of money? After all, you may have "bought into" the advice a friend gave you about which countries in Europe you should visit.

Let's look at the other side of the equation. Who (or what) sold you all those things you bought? In each case it might be different: a helpful person who counseled you through the buying process; a bored person who simply rang up your purchase; a Web site that enabled you to buy from your home; or a billboard that seized your attention and convinced you that what it advertised was worth spending money on.

So, before going any further, let's bring definition and structure to all these words we so often use.

TERMINOLOGY

Pretend you're working on a new dictionary. You need to formulate a definition of four very common phrases. Give a one-sentence definition for each:

1. To sell:

2. To serve:

3. To market:

4. The travel industry:

How did you do? Was it challenging? Almost surely it was. Indeed, some of the simplest words we use are the hardest to define. Let's take a look at how the experts might define each.

Selling

Selling is, at its most basic, **the act of offering things for purchase.** Note that this definition seems to imply very little skill or involvement on the part of the salesperson. In fact, it doesn't even *require* a person. A Web site, a newspaper ad, or a catalog can all offer goods or services for purchase. They do, in a sense, "sell." (Of course, there has to be someone who designed the message *behind* that **sell piece** [anything that helps promote and sell a product or service]. Perhaps he or she, in a way, is the salesperson.)

Selling, however, can be much more than merely facilitating a purchase. It can require deep knowledge, great skill, and a passion to provide the buyer with what he needs and/or wants. This higher level of personal selling is often called **consultative selling**. It can be defined as the act of **helping a person make a wise buying decision.** It focuses on the person's needs and how he or she can be satisfied by what you sell. As you'll see, it's an ideal model for selling travel products.

EVEN 2,000 YEARS AGO...

The sign typically found at the entrance to marketplaces in the Roman Empire: "Caveat Emptor." (Let the buyer beware).

This concept of focusing on the buyer's needs is today a popular one. Unfortunately, it wasn't always so. Until fairly recently, the landscape of sales was often littered with trickery, deceit, and manipulation. "Snake oil" salesmen claimed their medicines could cure anything. Merchants would sell jewelry that turned out to be fake. Prices would be adjusted according to how wealthy or gullible the customer appeared to be.

Do such dubious sales tactics still exist? To some extent, yes. Telemarketers who intentionally interrupt your dinner, auto "finance managers" who come up with all sorts of extra costs after you've bought your car, and merchants who play price games with you in an outdoor marketplace are all trying to make money at your expense. No wonder you might not like the thought of being called a salesperson.

But it doesn't have to be that way, especially in the travel business. Selling can and should be something you do *for* and *with* someone, not *to* someone. It can be an immensely rewarding and fulfilling career, as you'll discover in the pages ahead.

Service

Look back at your definition of *to serve*. It's an especially hard word to define. It has so many meanings. It could refer to someone who fixes your TV, as per your *service* contract. It could also simply indicate that something has been provided (as in "dinner is served").

Here's a definition, though, that's especially useful: **Service is the way a person and/or company interacts with and treats its customers.**

Servicepeople (who also may be salespeople; the two do often overlap) are what make buying and experiencing what you purchase a pleasant process. They're there when you need them. They're knowledgeable, well informed, caring, efficient, and strive for excellence. And they're friendly at all times.

Even a Web site can convey how a company interacts with and treats its customers. A well-designed site that's easy to navigate provides pleasant "virtual" service. A poorly conceived site irritates the buyer and may discourage present or future sales.

SERVICE MOMENTS IN THE TRAVEL INDUSTRY

- A hotel front-desk clerk welcomes you by name.
- A smiling flight attendant asks you if you'd like a pillow.
- A stateroom steward on a cruise ship turns down your bed while you're at dinner.
- A shuttle driver helps you with your luggage as you exit.
- A waitress at a themed restaurant asks if you'd like a refill for your coffee.
- A car rental employee listens to your complaint in a patient and understanding way, then offers a solution.
- An employee at a tourist bureau answers the phone as soon as it rings.
- A sales clerk at a travel bookstore locates the guidebook you've had trouble finding.
- A theme park employee gives directions to a ride.
- A travel agent asks what airline seating you prefer.

We'll look at service much more completely in Chapter 5. For now, just a few thoughts:

- To succeed, a salesperson must also have sharp service skills.
- To keep a company profitable, a serviceperson should have at least a few sales skills.
- Service opportunities potentially occur at many moments: while something is bought; while what is bought is being experienced or used; and even after the whole process is over (or at least seems to be). For example, a phone reservationist for a hotel chain can be especially gracious while a potential guest is asking questions; a housekeeper may arrange that guest's toiletries on a small towel on the bathroom sink; the hotel sends the customer a newsletter after his return.
- To succeed, a serviceperson must genuinely care about the satisfaction of the person whose needs he or she is serving.

Marketing

Look back to your definition of marketing. The greatest misconception about marketing is that it means just about the same thing as selling. The reality: Sales is but one step in the much broader phenomenon that marketing represents.

Here's a definition: **Marketing is the process of transferring a product from its producer to consumers.** But what is a **product? It's anything that's offered to people for purchase and that addresses their needs or**

wants. It can be a physical, tangible item (e.g., a set of luggage) or an abstract, intangible one (a vacation or even an idea).

Some economists limit the definition of a product to physical things you can own. When they refer to nonphysical things you don't own but experience, they use the word *service*. In this book, though, we'll avoid making a distinction between products and services. We'll use the broader definition of *product*, since people in the travel industry almost always call what they sell *travel products*, even if these products are intangibles.

To market a product, you must be prepared to research, develop, cost, sell, service, and follow up. At most companies, marketing is choreographed by management, rather than front-line sales- or servicepeople. However, some of the greatest marketing insights often come from front-liners—they do, after all, deal with customers on a direct, daily basis. Wise marketing managers pay close attention to front-line feedback. And in certain fields (especially travel), marketing executives often start out as sales- or servicepeople, working their way up through the company.

KINDS OF SELLING

As you've noticed, selling takes many forms. Let's follow an especially broad approach, one that fits well with the travel industry. This approach argues that four types of selling take place: **front-line-to-the-public, business-to-business, within-business,** and **nonpersonal selling.** The first three usually require people. The last one—as you can tell by its name—does not.

FRONT-LINE EMPLOYEES

Front-line employees are those who interact directly with the public on a regular basis. They may work in sales or in service. Some travel examples: reservationists, hotel front-desk personnel, airport skycaps, and travel agents.

1. Front-Line-to-the-Public Selling

This is perhaps the most obvious and familiar form of selling. **Front-line-to-the-public selling occurs when the customer and salesperson interact directly**—in person, on the phone, possibly by fax, or by e-mail, and soon, via a live camera feed on the Internet.

Based on your own travel planning experiences, try to come up with three examples of this type of front-line-to-the-public travel sales situation. Write them below. (We've come up with one scenario as an example to help you along):

EXAMPLE   You visit a travel agent at her office and talk to her about taking a tour of China. She asks you some well-focused questions, then recommends what she feels would be the right tour company for you. It sounds great. The price she quotes seems reasonable, too. You give her your credit card number to cover the deposit.

Your example #1:

Your example #2:

Your example #3:

   Look back at your examples. Was at least one of them phone-based? Good. A majority of today's front-line-to-the-public sales do take place over the telephone. Did you use examples from other sectors of the travel industry (that is, other than a travel agency situation)? If you did, it shows that you realize the full extent of possible seller-buyer scenarios in travel. For instance, you might have described how a car rental representative asked you if you'd like to upgrade to a full-size car or whether you'd be interested in purchasing their insurance protection plan. Though that representative's job is primarily a service one, the car rental firm's expectation is that he will do some selling, too.

WHAT DO YOU CALL THE BUYER?

The word *buyer* is a useful one in a textbook. In the business world, though, this term is rarely used. Most sectors of the travel industry favor the word *customer*. It's a good, useful term that applies to most situations.

However, certain industry segments utilize other descriptives, too. The lodging, cruise, and theme park industries often use the word *guests* to refer to their customers. Transportation providers—like airlines, motorcoach operators, and rail service providers—frequently describe their customers as *passengers* (sometimes abbreviated as **pax**). Destination Marketing Organizations and attractions regularly employ the term *visitors*. (A **destination marketing organization,** or **DMO,** is an organization that promotes destinations. A DMO that represents a country is usually called a **tourist bureau** or **tourist office.** When a DMO represents something smaller, like a city, it's often called a **convention and visitors bureau** or **CVB.**)

To emphasize the professional nature of their consulting services, travel agencies like to call their customers *clients*. And marketers in all segments utilize *prospects* to refer to potential customers and *the public* for potential buyers who aren't in a business-to-business sales situation.

---

2. Business-to-Business Selling

This type of interpersonal selling is one of the most important in any industry. Indeed, it's the *only* kind of sales that some businesses conduct. **In the business-to-business model, one company sells to another company, not to the public.** (Some companies sell to both other companies *and* directly to the public.) Here are a few examples from the travel industry, often representing "package" situations:

- A motorcoach company rents its vehicles to a tour company.
- A Web site design firm sells its services to a tourist bureau.
- A travel agency provides travel arrangements for a corporation's employees.
- A hotel sells space to a meeting planning company.
- A charter airline leases an aircraft to a tour operator.
- An insurance company that specializes in travel coverage insures a cruise line against possible mishaps.
- An attraction sells admission tickets to a tour operator.

Most of these are **hard sales** situations, **ones in which one company sells a product to another.** The company that bought these products either incorporates them into its own product or resells them to the public, acting as an intermediary between the original business and the public.

There are also **soft** business-to-business sales situations. **Soft selling occurs when no actual product is being purchased—the goal is simply to reinforce the seller-buyer relationship and to lay a foundation for future sales.** For instance, productive travel agencies are often visited by sales representatives from major travel companies, like tour operators, cruise lines, airlines and car rental companies. The sales rep "sells" the quality and value of the organization she represents to these agencies. She also makes herself available to the agencies by phone, fax, or e-mail, in the event that they have needs to be met.

TRAVEL DISTRIBUTION

There are two ways to make travel products available. In the **direct** model, **suppliers** (what most companies in the travel business are called) **sell directly to the public.** This is called **retailing.** In the **indirect** method, **suppliers sell through intermediaries,** who also may be called suppliers (e.g., tour operators) or can be seen as distributors only (e.g., travel agencies). Here, the intermediaries are the retailers and the original suppliers are **wholesalers** (since they sell something to a business for resale).

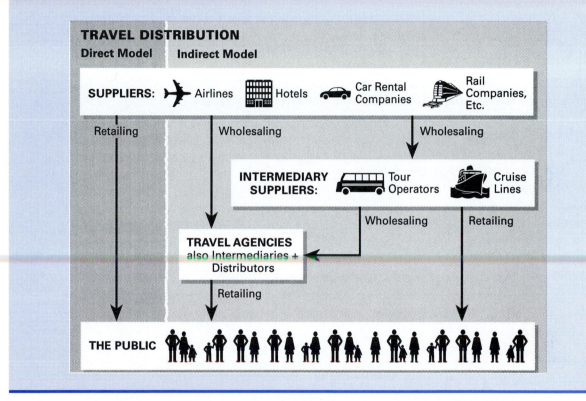

So, to summarize, a sales rep's mission is to:

- *Inform* travel agents, tour operators, and others of the product he or she represents and convince them of its value.
- *Educate* these people on how to sell those products.
- *Resolve* any questions or problems that may arise.
- *Motivate* people to sell the rep's products more frequently and with greater commitment.

In other words, a sales representative functions both as a salesperson and as a service provider. Above all, he or she—like any good salesperson—nurtures the relationship between the supplier and such intermediaries as travel agencies (which help distribute that supplier's products to the public). The rep, through soft selling, becomes the "face" of an otherwise impersonal corporation.

Business-to-business selling isn't just limited to supplier and intermediary situations. In some cases *organizations,* rather than companies, do the soft selling. For instance, a tourist bureau isn't really a company. It's an *organization.* It doesn't exist, like a company does, to make money. Yet tourist bureaus regularly try to "sell" their destinations to tour companies, cruise lines, and travel agencies. "Why not plan an itinerary stop for your tour at our destination," they say, "or use our ports, or recommend us to your clients?" This is indeed a form of soft selling. (DMOs, through advertising, "sell" directly to the public, too.)

SALES REPS BY ANY OTHER NAME

Among the terms used in the travel industry to describe sales reps:

- District sales managers (DSMs)
- Business development managers
- Business development representatives
- Sales managers
- Account executives
- National account directors
- Field sales managers
- Regional sales managers
- Regional sales directors

3. Within-Business Selling

Let's stretch the definition of selling even more. It's often critically important to sell *an idea* within a company. Perhaps the manager of a travel agency wants to convince her travel counselors that more flexible hours would serve them—and their clients—much more effectively. The itinerary planner for a tour operator may wish to recommend that Prague be added to his company's *Glittering Capitals of Europe* tour. The vice president of a lodging chain may want to convince the company's president and board of directors that they should start up an all-suite division of their brand's lodging mix. And the human resources director at a theme park may wish to convince employees that the safety training they undergo is valuable and necessary.

In each case, the very same arsenal of techniques that a front-liner uses will help these people win over the hearts and minds of others in their company. They understand that what helps a company sell to **external**

customers (the buying public) works equally well with their **internal customers**—those people they work with and must sell ideas to.

4. Nonpersonal Selling

Up to now, we've only examined **personal selling,** where one person sells to another. But businesses also sell through **nonpersonal** channels, such as advertising.

Some examples: billboards, brochures, Web sites, and TV ads. In such cases, the idea is to motivate the consumer to buy the product with no sales*person* doing the convincing. Customers may even purchase and book the product without any human intervention at all: on the Internet, by mailing in a completed form with a check, or through some other non-personal medium.

Of course, that no sales- or serviceperson is involved is only partially true. An *army* of marketing and sales experts may have conceived that billboard ad. Hundreds of people will process those bookings. And a TV commercial may feature a celebrity who "sells" that trip to you.

Again, nonpersonal selling uses many of the same tactics that salespeople deploy. Let's find out what those techniques are and how the sales cycle in travel typically unfolds.

This Pleasant Holidays ad is typical of a newspaper advertising piece. *(Courtesy of Pleasant Holidays)*

THE SALES CYCLE

Think of the last time you went to a store to buy a pair of shoes. Now outline below every action that took place, from the moment you entered the store to the moment when you left after buying your shoes:

You've probably just described a typical sales cycle. Here are the steps that most businesses utilize to make a sale:

1. *Welcoming:* Greeting a customer at the first moment of the sales interaction.
2. *Determining needs:* Asking questions to assess what needs a client has. (This is often referred to as *qualifying* or *interviewing*.)
3. *Recommending solutions:* Communicating what products will satisfy the client's needs.
4. *Addressing concerns:* Finding solutions to any misconceptions or hesitance a customer may have to buying your recommendation.
5. *Enhancing the sale:* Recommending additional and/or better products that will provide a more fulfilling experience for the client.
6. *Achieving an agreement:* When the buyer and seller agree to the recommendations that will "solve" the customer's needs. Often called *closing*, this step usually marks the point when the customer financially commits to buying the product.

These generic steps work in almost every sales situation and with almost any product, service, or idea. Let's return to our shoe sales scenario and see how it fits the cycle just described.

Almost surely when you walk into the store a salesperson welcomes you. He probably asks you a few questions about what your needs are. A casual shoe? A dress shoe? What size do you wear? What price range do you have in mind? He then recommends one or two shoe models that will "solve" your needs. You like one pair, but you worry that the shoes feel a little tight. He addresses your concern by checking where your toe is in the shoe and concludes that the stretching that always occurs with this shoe model will, within a few days, solve the tightness problem. You agree to buy the shoes he recommends. He suggests that you also buy a shoe tree to slide into the shoes when not in use. This will help them keep their shape and extend their life. Sounds good to you. He rings up the sale and thanks you for buying from him. A few weeks later he sends a postcard to you reaffirming his appreciation.

SALES CYCLE SYNONYMS

Though the sales cycle depicted is a universally accepted one, the terms used to describe each step vary. Here are some other descriptives you may hear:

Our term	Alternatives
1. Welcoming	Greeting, opening, starting the sale, approaching, acknowledging the customer, making a connection, creating a link, building rapport, identifying the client, establishing rapport
2. Determining needs	Qualifying, interviewing, questioning, probing, investigating, asking questions, assessing the situation, understanding needs, finding out needs, gathering information, obtaining information, identifying needs, seeking information, uncovering needs
3. Recommending solutions	Presenting recommendations, delivering your ideas, proposing recommendations, linking solutions to needs, sharing knowledge, informing, making a sales presentation, matching needs with products, satisfying needs, sharing what you know, analyzing options, solving needs
4. Addressing concerns	Countering objections, solving objections, overcoming obstacles, handling objections, overcoming resistance, reducing resistance, countering concerns, dealing with obstacles, resolving roadblocks, providing reassurance, overcoming objections, overcoming barriers, responding to concerns
5. Enhancing the sale	Upselling/cross-selling, adding value, making additional recommendations
6. Achieving an agreement	Closing, getting the business, testing the interest, asking for the sale, earning a commitment, motivating to action, asking for the business, landing the account, asking for the commitment, making the sale, obtaining commitment
7. Following up	Ensuring satisfaction, remembering the client, showing appreciation, obtaining feedback

   Throughout this book we'll emphasize the phrases in the left-hand column, since they convey the sales and service attitude that works so well in the travel business. Expect some of the phrases on the right, too. The reason: to remind you that these terms are commonly used, as well.

   Our shoe scenario—and the sales cycle it reflects—applies extremely well to selling travel. We've also carefully chosen a terminology that fits the travel environment. The terms you've just learned emphasize integrity, reinforce credibility, respect the customers' needs, engage them in the sales process, and help ensure that both seller and buyer will benefit. Whenever a high degree of trust is needed (travelers need to feel that the salesperson has their welfare in mind) and the client is investing a great deal of money on a future travel experience, the sale must be about relationships, not trickery or manipulation.

WHO USES EACH STEP IN THE SALES CYCLE?

Sales step	Who uses it
1. Welcoming	All salespeople
2. Determining needs	Transactional salespeople—people who are primarily order-takers—use certain questions (limited, *vanguard* or closed-ended questions) to obtain logistic information. Consultative salespeople—people who analyze a client's logistic *and* deeper needs—use both vanguard and more open-ended *explorer* questions. (More about this in Chapter 2.)
3. Recommending solutions	All salespeople, with more complex or subtle solutions coming in consultative situations
4. Addressing concerns	All salespeople
5. Enhancing the sale	All salespeople. At one time, transactional salespeople rarely did this. It has now become standard practice for them, however.
6. Achieving an agreement	All salespeople, though the agreement in a transactional situation may be a simple fulfillment of the buyer's logistic needs.
7. Following up	Transactional salespeople rarely follow up, though the company they work for may. Consultative salespeople should always follow up.

WHY TRAVELERS BUY

Do people *need* to travel? We do use that word all the time. Yet, technically, people only need food, shelter and clothing—the *essentials* of life. Anything else is **discretionary—products acquired because the person *chooses* to do so.** Discretionary items are things that are desired but not essential to living. (Most economists call a discretionary item a **want,** rather than a need.) Travel certainly fits that description.

WHAT'S TRAVEL?

Earlier in this chapter, we asked you to define *sales, service, marketing,* and, yes, the *travel industry* itself. The last one may have been the most difficult one of all. The reason: The travel industry encompasses so much.

Even travel professionals argue about the meaning of *travel* and its allied terminology. Some define travel simply: *the act of journeying from one place to another.* It's a safe definition, one that's very all-inclusive. For industry purposes, of course, it would exclude traveling within your community for everyday purposes, like going to the supermarket. There's something special—not everyday—about travel.

You'll often hear the word *tourism,* as well. Some argue that it's simply a synonym for travel. Others believe that *travel* should apply only to *modes* of travel (air, rail, motorcoach, etc.), while *tourism* embraces the entire business, including non*travel* elements, like lodging, dining, theme parks, destination promotion, and the like. Most people avoid the whole issue and refer to the "travel and tourism industry."

And what's *transportation?* This term refers not only to moving people, but also things, like cargo. And *hospitality?* It describes those products and services that accommodate, entertain and feed people, including lodging, restaurants, attractions, and theme parks.

Bottom line: This terminology can be quite slippery. There are no absolute, agreed-upon boundaries to what each word means.

Yet for many of us today, travel is almost a necessity. Without it, you may feel overstressed, understimulated, and somehow empty. With it, you feel energized, enriched, and perhaps relaxed (even though travel certainly can be quite exhausting). Even in times of national stress—as when a major terrorist act occurs—people find safe ways to vacation within a matter of weeks or months. Within a year, normal travel patterns largely resume.

How travel benefits people, though, varies from person to person, even from trip to trip. Let's explore why *you* travel. Imagine you will soon be taking your dream vacation. Oh yes, and you just won the lottery. Now fill in the following:

- My dream vacation will be to the following destination:

- I would like the following person(s) to go with me (you can also go alone):

- I will stay for the following amount of time:

- I will go during the following month:

- I'll see my destination by (choose one): car rental, tour, cruise, train or other:

Now ask yourself: "Why did I complete the above sentences like I did? What might I get out of this vacation?" For example, if you were taking a business trip (which wouldn't fit the *leisure travel* scenario we described), it might be to get new business, visit customers, make money, feel good about your importance to your company, and travel with a minimal amount of hassles.

So go back to your dream vacation. List the *three principal reasons* why you chose the vacation you did:

1.

2.

3.

Compare what you wrote with the following list of typical motives that people have for buying leisure travel:

1. To have fun
2. For excitement
3. To relax, unwind, and get away from responsibilities and stress
4. For adventure
5. To do or experience something new
6. To learn about history, culture, the arts, nature, etc.
7. To meet new people
8. To visit friends or relatives (usually abbreviated as VFR)
9. To see a famous place or attraction you've heard about
10. To practice a certain sport or other activity (eg., diving, skiing, golfing, etc.)
11. To pursue a special interest or hobby
12. For a romantic experience (e.g., a honeymoon)
13. To reward yourself for an achievement or milestone (e.g., a wedding anniversary)
14. To sample great cuisine
15. To shop and buy interesting things
16. To gamble
17. To do something nice for the person who's traveling with you (e.g., your family)
18. For religious purposes
19. To pamper yourself
20. To break away from everyday routine

Did your reasons fit into any of the above categories? In all probability, they did. You should, however, realize the following about buyers' motives:

1. **How much discretionary money you have and what proportion of it you're willing to spend on travel will have an enormous impact on your decision.** If you had been told that you had only $2,000 to spend, your choice would have been quite different from the one in the lottery scenario.
2. **Some buying decisions are so psychologically deep that most people don't readily acknowledge them.** For example, some people might choose a certain trip because it reinforces their sense of prestige or worth, and heightens the image other people have of them.
3. **In most people, at least a few counterforces may offset the desire to travel.** Three examples: A fear of certain modes of transportation (e.g., flying); guilt about spending money on something nonessential; and discomfort with unfamiliar places, foods, lodgings, etc. These counterforces can be so great that they prevent certain people from ever going on vacation. In others, it channels choices toward comfortable, familiar, or safe travel decisions. Seeing California by tour, for example, feels far more acceptable to timid people than doing it on their own.
4. **Motives for travel vary from person to person, even for the same trip.** One person might want to visit the Bahamas to go diving, another to shop, a third to unwind, and a fourth to learn about the people. Same place, different motives.
5. **Motives can change for the same person, depending on the trip.** This year you may want to visit Cancun just to lie on the beach all day and "veg out." Next trip, though, you may wish to spend twelve days in Europe in constant activity, exploration, and learning.

These five insights are hugely important if you intend to sell travel. Any salesperson who seeks genuine excellence pushes beyond the obvious conclusions to reach an understanding of customers that is deep and meaningful.

LEARNING FROM OPPOSITES

Contrasts often help us better understand just about any topic. So let's examine some opposites in selling and discover how they shed light on selling travel.

Tangibles vs. Intangibles

Buying a car, a computer, underwear, or donuts is fundamentally different from buying stock, an insurance policy, a tennis lesson, or a vacation. The first list is composed of **tangibles;** the second, **intangibles.**

We've talked about tangibles and intangibles already, but let's now define them. **Tangibles are things you can see and touch; intangibles are things you can't see or touch.** As author Harry Beckwith puts it, when you're selling intangibles, you're "selling the invisible."

WHY PEOPLE TAKE CRUISES

Cruises have become immensely popular. Why? Because a cruise...

A cruise ship sails in Alaska. *(Courtesy of Holland America Line)*

- Encourages you to relax and get away from it all
- Allows you to be pampered
- Gives you the chance to visit several geographical areas/destinations
- Represents good value for the money
- Offers a variety of activities
- Affords a good way to try out a vacation area that you might want to return to
- Represents a fun vacation
- Allows you to do as much or as little as you want
- Features high-quality entertainment
- Offers comfortable accommodations
- Saves you from the need to repeatedly pack and unpack
- Provides a way to meet interesting people
- Represents a learning experience
- Affords a romantic getaway

Source: Cruise Lines International Association (CLIA)

No one would take a cruise for *all* these motives. Each person has a particular subset of motives, perhaps three or four, which speaks to them in an especially powerful way.

That travel is an intangible (i.e., you can buy a cruise, but you won't be buying the ship) has many repercussions. Because travel is an intangible, you must help your clients imagine themselves on the vacation. For example, since they can't actually experience the trip before going, they can't "test drive" it, as they would a car. In essence, they buy it sight unseen. You'll learn many more implications of the intangible nature of traveling in future chapters—and how to adjust your sales, service, and marketing strategies accordingly.

Perishable vs. Nonperishable Products

When a product has a "long shelf life"—when it keeps its value over a long time—it's said to have low or nonperishability. It still retains its value, whether it's sold or not. Of course, all products eventually lose value. After a year in the showroom, a car or a big-screen TV set will eventually be marked down to make way for new models.

Travel products, however, are highly perishable. They lose all value if not sold when they "happen." If, for example, an airline doesn't sell a seat on a flight, a hotel doesn't fill a hotel room on a certain day, or a tour departs with ten empty seats on the motorcoach, the possibility to sell those seats or rooms *is gone forever*.

How do travel providers deal with the perishability of their products?

- **They reduce the price frequently,** if necessary, as the "expiration date" approaches (like what supermarkets do with their own perishable goods, such as bread, bagels, and bananas).
- **They use multiple channels to move their products.** An airline, for example, sells directly, through travel agents, through **consolidators** (companies that sell special inventories of products at highly discounted rates) and, in a sense, through cruise lines and tour operators.
- **Some suppliers (airlines, hotels, and car rental companies) overbook:** They use computer models to predict the number of no-shows (based on past patterns) and sell more seats, rooms, or car rentals than they actually have. If all goes right, a minimal number of their product will go unused. (If their predictions go wrong and an "oversold" situation occurs, then some customers are sure to be unhappy.)

Commodities vs. Experiences

Commodity is a slippery word to define. You may have heard of the commodities exchange, where things like gold, corn, and pork bellies (of all things) are bought and sold. Commodities can also refer to mass-produced, unspecialized products, like pencils, tube socks, nails, extension cords, and masking tape.

In the travel business, however, **commodities often refer to products that are simple, similar to one other, and often bought based on price alone.** The classic example: a flight. If you want to go from Los Angeles to Orlando, you know that the flight, whether it's on United or Delta, will vary little. The planes of each carrier will go the same speed, along the same route, with the same kind of seats, legroom, level of efficiency, and service. Assuming all other factors are equal (both have similar availability, departure time, and type of aircraft), you'll probably decide which one to book based on price alone.

To overcome this *sameness of product* (marketers call it **parity**), airlines use all sorts of sales, service, and marketing tactics: their logos, slogans, even the paint on their planes are saying "we're different!" But are they really? Does "Fly the friendly skies" really mean anything? It's also significant that the airlines needed to create frequent-flyer programs that award free travel for mileage flown. This is all because of the commodity nature of the flight experience. (In a few cases, real differences between airlines do exist, but let's keep it simple for now.)

Other travel products, like tours and cruises, are at the opposite end of the scale. They're less commodities than **experiences: they're complex, different from one another and often are bought based on factors much more complicated than price.** A Carnival cruise is totally different from a Cruise West journey. A Contiki tour is very dissimilar from a Trafalgar tour. To sell such experiences requires great knowledge, patience, insight, and skill.

The difference between a travel commodity and a travel experience has all sorts of implications. Here's one: If you want to buy an air ticket, you really don't need much help (or at least you think you don't). That's why the leading travel products sold on the Internet are flights. If you want to take a cruise or a tour, however, you usually need the personal guidance of someone like a travel agent. (Unless you've cruised or toured so often that you deeply understand the suppliers involved.) Choosing the wrong cruise or tour—one that doesn't fit your needs, personality, and style—would be a costly mistake. That's why only a small percentage of cruises and tours are sold through the Internet. Most (about 90 percent) are booked through travel agents.

Many products fall somewhere between a commodity and an experience. Lodging is one example. In reality, hotels are actually much more like experiences, with important distinctions among brands and even individual hotels. Yet, for complex reasons, the public seems to view lodging more like a commodity. This "pulls" the lodging sector closer to a midpoint on the commodity-experience scale. And, tellingly, it's at a midpoint among Internet travel sales, too.

Transactional vs. Consultative Selling

Let's circle back to the opening pages of this chapter. You learned that selling can be more than just facilitating a purchase. Yet in some cases that's not true. When it's all that you're doing—making it possible for someone to buy something—it's called **transactional selling.** Your role is largely that of an order-taker, your goal to transact. It requires minimal skill and only basic qualifying: You find out who, what, when, where, how much, and how long. That's about it. In fact, to your employer, your service skills may be more valuable than your sales skills.

Consultative selling, on the other hand, is much closer to the model we will discuss in the three chapters that follow. It requires sharper skills and deeper understanding—and usually turns out to be more fulfilling and rewarding. It implies a career, not a job.

Very often, it's the nature of what you sell that determines whether you'll transact or consult. *Commodities lend themselves to transactional selling, but experiences are best sold through a consultative approach.* Does an airline reservationist need to know the deeper motives of someone who calls? Probably not. But does a travel agent need to understand the needs and desires of a client before fashioning a two-week vacation to South America for him? You bet. Business-to-business salespeople need to be consultative, too. And how about reservationists for hotels, car rental firms, cruise companies, and tour operators? Though they can manage by remaining transactional, callers do sometimes need help in making the right choice. Reservationists, then, have to become somewhat consultative—asking questions, making recommendations, etc.—before they can get the caller's business.

One final and very important thought: *It's very easy to fall into transactional selling, even if you should be selling consultatively.* It's a lot easier for, say, a travel agent to be simply an order-taker—arrange what the client asks for, and that's that. The problem: This sort of agent won't build a valuable, loyalty-generating relationship with the agency's customers or maximize the profitability and potential client satisfaction with the trip. Just remember: You don't really make a profit on a transaction. You make a profit on a customer. That's where the focus should be.

Another factor: *Computers and the Internet are superb transactors.* The days may be numbered for transactional salespeople, even for those who are highly skilled at transactional travel selling. Then again, those transactors who can also apply sales techniques along the way may increase their value to their companies and therefore survive, even thrive.

The future for fully consultative salespeople, however, should remain bright. Automated systems aren't nimble or trusted enough to handle consultative selling. Maybe "artificial intelligence" computer programs will someday succeed at simulating consultative selling. But don't expect that to happen for a long time.

SOME CONCLUDING THOUGHTS

Done accurately, enthusiastically, and with good intent, serving, selling, and marketing to the traveling public can be an immensely rewarding experience. In the chapters that follow, you'll learn the precise strategies and skills to connect with those travel customers of yours.

Name:_____   Date:_____

ACTIVITY #1   WHAT'S YOUR SALES AND SERVICE IQ?

If you're already a salesperson, the following self-analysis will help you gauge your skills. If you're not yet a salesperson, it'll give you a snapshot of your potential. In either case, you'll learn where your strengths are and in which areas you need improvement.

Guidelines: 1 = always; 2 = usually; 3 = sometimes; 4 = rarely; 5 = never

I consider myself:	Always ⟵			⟶ Never
1. Outgoing	1	2	3	4	5
2. Honest	1	2	3	4	5
3. Persistent	1	2	3	4	5
4. Focused	1	2	3	4	5
5. Punctual	1	2	3	4	5
6. Neat	1	2	3	4	5
7. Confident	1	2	3	4	5
8. Positive	1	2	3	4	5
9. A good listener	1	2	3	4	5
10. A problem solver	1	2	3	4	5
11. A good learner	1	2	3	4	5
12. Thorough	1	2	3	4	5
13. Sensitive	1	2	3	4	5
14. Enthusiastic	1	2	3	4	5
15. A people person	1	2	3	4	5
16. Prompt at follow-up	1	2	3	4	5
17. Thoughtful	1	2	3	4	5
18. A good communicator	1	2	3	4	5
19. Courteous	1	2	3	4	5
20. Considerate	1	2	3	4	5

Scoring:

80–100: You have a very strong sales/service personality

60–79: You're well suited to sales and service

40–59: You'll need to work on your sales and service

Under 40: Sales and service will be a challenge for you, but you can do it

Now, in the space below, write those traits (by their numbers) that you think are primarily sales-related and those that largely deal with service.

Sales   **Service**

Name:_____ Date:_____

ACTIVITY #2   CRUISING ALONG

Here are the "why cruise" motives we gave you earlier from CLIA's consumer survey. In the space below, write in the reasons that would motivate you to take a cruise, in the order of importance to *you*. Add any that CLIA might have missed.

- Encourages you to relax and get away from it all
- Allows you to be pampered
- Gives you the chance to visit several geographical areas/destinations
- Represents good value for the money
- Offers a variety of activities
- Affords a good way to try out a vacation area that you might want to return to
- Represents a fun vacation
- Allows you to do as much or as little as you want
- Features high-quality entertainment
- Offers comfortable accommodations
- Saves you from the need to repeatedly pack and unpack
- Provides a way to meet interesting people
- Represents a learning experience
- Affords a romantic getaway

Your list:

1.

2.

3.

What can you conclude from the similarities and differences between your list and CLIA's?

Name:_____ Date:_____

ACTIVITY #3 SURFING THE VIRTUAL WORLD

Destinations "sell" themselves, too. And the Internet has become a prime way for them to do so. Explore the following destinations' through their promotional Web sites.

- Great Britain: *www.visitbritain.com*
- The Bahamas: *www.bahamas.com*
- Australia: *www.australia.com*

Rate each with a letter grade (A to F), according to the indicated criteria:

1. *www.visitbritain.com*

___ Attractiveness of home page (first one you see)

___ Ease of navigating the site

___ Ability to find things you're interested in

___ Ability to convey what the destination experience is like

___ Ability to entice you to go there

2. *www.bahamas.com*

___ Attractiveness of home page (first one you see)

___ Ease of navigating the site

___ Ability to find things you're interested in

___ Ability to convey what the destination experience is like

___ Ability to entice you to go there

3. *www.australia.com*

___ Attractiveness of home page (first one you see)

___ Ease of navigating the site

___ Ability to find things you're interested in

___ Ability to convey what the destination experience is like

___ Ability to entice you to go there

2
Welcoming Customers and Determining Their Needs

OBJECTIVES

After reading this chapter, you'll be able to:

- Apply twelve techniques for effectively welcoming customers

- Determine needs according to the customer's situation

- Practice the seven secrets of great client interviews

- Conduct effective prospecting

Think of your best friend. Way back, what was your very first impression of him or her? Write a description of your original feelings in the space below and give the reasons why you arrived at that impression:

The person: _____

Your first impression:

Now two key questions: Was your initial impression made quickly? Has it changed over time in any fundamental way?

If you're like most people, you came to a conclusion about your friend *very quickly*. Indeed, several studies have demonstrated that most people decide what they think of a person in about *six seconds*. Unfortunate, unfair, but usually true.

In all probability, your initial impression has evolved over the years into something based less on superficials and more on the deeper, more complex qualities of your friend's personality. But it takes time, lots of time, for that to happen.

This has enormous implications for selling and serving customers, because in sales, the first impression you make will be a lasting one. Salespeople and, especially, servicepeople have too little contact time with customers for a fully developed impression to form.

So those first few seconds are exceedingly important. Moreover, customers aren't just formulating a conclusion about you. *They're coming to a conclusion about the entire business you represent*. If a hotel's front-desk clerk is attentive, gracious and kind, you'll conclude that this hotel really cares. If a travel agent greets you on the phone with energy and enthusiasm, you'll decide that she really will help you fashion a wonderful trip. If you walk into a meeting to pitch your new itinerary idea, your posture, eye contact, and upbeat attitude will set the stage for a positive, productive session.

WAL-MART LOVES YOU

Wal-Mart has, for decades, been a very profitable company. Many experts attribute at least part of this success to Wal-Mart's official greeters.

When you walk into a Wal-Mart, a smiling someone is usually there at the door to say hello and ask if you need help. It's a small but striking gesture, one that sets the tone for your shopping experience and that positions Wal-Mart as a friendly, caring company.

Of course, Wal-Mart has to follow through. If the servicepeople whom you interact with after the greeter are unhelpful or hard to find, then your initial positive impression will erode. Yet even that erosion will take time—lots of it—before it affects your attitude. Researchers have proved that the initial impression will fade only if many negative experiences occur over a long period.

GREAT IN-PERSON WELCOMES

Think of the last three things you bought. Write them below and indicate *how* you purchased them. In person? Over the phone? From a catalog? On the Internet? In some other way?

What you bought   *The way you bought it*

1.

2.

3.

If you're like most people, you are "time-starved." You just don't have the time to buy everything in person. That's why you *probably* purchased at least two of the things you listed above over the phone or the Internet. Even meals from restaurants aren't always bought in person: We telephone for pizza deliveries and drive up to a speaker box at McDonald's to order a Big Mac. (Yes, you give your money to a person, but you *bought* through the speaker.)

But the most productive and powerful sales occur in a person-to-person environment. For example, it's twice as likely that people will buy a trip if they physically visit a travel agency, rather than call. The visual clues, more complex personal interactions, and clearer buyer commitment that an in-person visit implies all conspire to make that sale come true.

A welcome launches that in-person sales and service experience. Here are twelve ways you can carry out great in-person greetings, as well as what you should do in the immediate moments that follow that welcome. Remember, too, that many of these techniques intertwine quite tightly with *service* skills. You'll see some of them again in Chapter 5.

1. Make Quick, Friendly Eye Contact with the Customer

Some people feel uncomfortable about meeting someone's gaze. It feels so intimate. But in a buying context, it's interpreted simply as friendliness. Eye contact implies a commitment to pay attention, to help, and to serve. So smile, look straight at them, and show you care. (Think about places you've entered for assistance and nobody acknowledged your presence. Felt awful, didn't it?) Of course, we're not talking about staring (keeping eye contact too long, often without smiling). Keep it friendly.

If making eye contact isn't natural to you, here's a little trick: Make a point of immediately determining the eye color of every person you meet. Eye contact will become natural, automatic, and easy.

2. Stand Up

To stand up when someone arrives is a vital gesture. It shows that you respect the customer. It conveys that you're ready to take action on his or her behalf. It puts you on a more equal level—the client isn't "looking down" at you. This is important, especially in consultative selling, where buyers want to sense that they're dealing with professionals, people at the same level as them, but in an altogether different field.

FOREIGN GAZES

In many countries, eye contact is a friendly gesture. But not everywhere. Many people in the Caribbean, for example, perceive eye contact and immediate smiles as suspicious. Why would someone you don't know instantly be warm to you? What are they up to? This sort of thing should be reserved for friends, they feel, not for people you don't know who pass briefly through your life and job.

As a result, for many years visitors to, say, Jamaica, would return with an impression that Jamaicans disliked tourists. Jamaicans seemed unconcerned, unfriendly, even hostile. In a few cases that may have been true. But usually it was simply a matter of **cultural dissonance, where two societies have different values and behaviors that lead to misinterpretation on one or both sides.**

Today, most travel-related employees in the Caribbean (and many other countries where similar values exist) have had enough experience and training to recognize and understand what's going on. Far more tourists now return from the Caribbean feeling that the people there are just wonderful, as it should be.

3. Shake Hands

In many societies, people greet with hugs and kisses, even with people they don't know well. Not in ours. To us, physical contact is inappropriate and may even border on harassment.

One physical contact gesture, though, is acceptable to most people: the handshake. In a society starved for physical contact, like ours, a handshake is a cogent gesture, one that signals cooperation and trust.

Your handshake should be firm, not limp, or vise-like. A "milquetoast" handshake communicates ineffectualness. An "I am Conan" or "I am Xena" handshake implies that you're trying to overpower your customer. Something in between is just right.

4. Use a Natural Greeting Phrase

"Hello, how may I help you?" is probably best, since it's friendly yet a bit formal. Note that it's "*how* may I help you?" not "may I help you?" "May I help you?" is a rather senseless phrase, because the client's answer is almost surely "yes." "How may I help you?" is a much more open phrase that invites a world of possibilities.

5. Smile!

Here's an old saying: "Don't open a shop unless you know how to smile." A smile is highly effective and virtually required in today's retail world. It makes you, the seller, feel better and it's contagious (it makes the buyer want to smile, too).

6. Think of the Buyer As an Old Friend

We all go through times when the last thing we want is for a customer to walk through the door. It's an interruption. But if an old friend came in, wouldn't you feel differently?

Clients aren't the enemy. In fact, they're people who very much want to like you, trust you, and pay you for help. They deserve warm and immediate attention.

7. If Necessary, Tell Them You'll Be Right with Them

This is one of the most important gestures of all. Most people hate being ignored, especially when they're about to spend a lot on a travel experience. Pause with whatever you're doing that can't be immediately interrupted and acknowledge the customer. Tell him that you, or someone, will be with him momentarily. Later, thank him for his patience.

8. Invite Them to Sit Next to You

Sitting opposite someone at a desk is a bit adversarial. Physically and symbolically you're on opposite sides. If it's possible (it's not if you're working at, say, a counter), ask your client to sit to the side of your desk. It will create a much friendlier environment.

9. Use the Client's Name

Someone once said, "There's nothing sweeter than the sound of one's own name." Find out your customer's name very early on and use it occasionally through the rest of the sales or service cycle. If you're in a transactional or service situation, use the person's family name (e.g., Mr. Robinson). If you're in a consultative situation, using the person's first name is usually appropriate. (Some experts argue that you should start with the person's family name and later shift to the first name if it feels comfortable to do so.)

Don't overuse a person's name, though. It will feel artificial both to you and to the customer. The three best times to use it: Early on; when you start giving your recommendations; and near when you're about to ask them for their business.

Remember, too, that many cultures are uncomfortable with using first names in a business situation, unless you know the person very well. These cultures also put great emphasis on using titles (e.g., Professor Heimlich, not Mr. Heimlich).

SOME EXAMPLES IN THE TRAVEL INDUSTRY OF USING A PERSON'S NAME

- On super-luxury cruise ships, the staff and crew get together on the first cruise night to study pictures of every passenger (usually from their passport photos). They memorize them and address each guest by name beginning the next morning.
- Some very upscale hotels have a camera at their front desks that take pictures of guests as they check in. The photos are then reproduced on sheets of paper, with names, so every staff member can memorize them. To the guests' pleasant surprise, people they've never dealt with before, including maitre d's, bellmen, and housekeepers, will say hello to them by name.
- In most hotels today, when you call from your room to someone working at the hotel (e.g., the operator or room service), your name appears on a little screen on their phone. This is to enable staff to acknowledge you by name.

Before going on to our tenth technique, do the following. What do you think is the most powerful word in the English language? Don't cheat! Don't look ahead. Write your guess in the space below:

Now it's time to find out.

10. Use the Most Powerful Word

A study at Yale University identified the most powerful, results-creating words and phrases in the English language (and probably any language, too). Here they are, in reverse order:

5. I'm proud of you.
4. What do you think?
3. Would you please . . . ?
2. Thank you.
1. You . . .

An obvious pattern, don't you think? All five have the word *you*. By the way, this textbook uses the word *you* 1,982 times.

11. Echo Their Words, Mirror Their Mood

This technique is a subtle and challenging one, but it works. People like people who use the same vocabulary as they do. For example, if the client refers to her "child," use the word *child*. If she says "kid," though, do the same. And avoid any phrases that your generation uses but that your *client's generation* doesn't. *Far out, cool,* and *dude* imply that you're stuck in a particular age group—the assumption will be that you won't understand your client's generation.

In fact, take a moment to try to find at least three words that you use all the time but that another generation doesn't. Write them here:

Now you have a list of words that you shouldn't use in sales and service situations! Note: Certain phrases are also a little too casual as well as being age-specific. An example: *You guys.* No matter what gender the clients are, try not to use it.

Echoing and mirroring can take many different forms. For example, if the customer seems to be a no-nonsense type, keep the sale tight and to the point. If the client is more easygoing, relax and be the same. If the client leans toward you, lean toward him. Remember: The best salespeople are psychological chameleons. They mimic the environment the client creates.

You can also take control of mirroring. When your client's body language is closed and tight, you can relax her by slowly going from your own "closed" position to an "open" one. Your client will probably mirror your posture and relax.

12. Cultivate a Neat, Professional Appearance and Environment

Why do some companies require uniforms or dress codes of their front-liners? To project an image—a professional, company-controlled image. In other cases, you'll find yourself in a situation where your attire is left to you—even though there will be definite but unspoken expectations.

Customers do judge a book by its cover. That's why you must be well dressed and well groomed.

Your appearance is just part of a larger picture, of a **greater variety of cues that shape the overall impression.** Marketers call these factors **atmospheres.** Atmospheres also encompass such things as the neatness of your workspace, the comfort of the seat your clients sit in, lighting, office sounds, and much more. Some of these you can't control. Others you can. Be keenly alert to what your customers experience when they meet you. It's all part of your welcome.

Do these twelve techniques apply only to front-line service- and sales-people? Let's find out. Below is a recap of all twelve. Now pretend you're the president of Southwest Airlines. You're about to meet a major stockholder. Which would apply to you? Circle the appropriate response for each.

1. Make quick, friendly eye contact	Applicable	Not applicable
2. Stand up	Applicable	Not applicable
3. Shake hands	Applicable	Not applicable
4. Use a natural greeting phrase	Applicable	Not applicable
5. Smile	Applicable	Not applicable
6. Think of them as an old friend	Applicable	Not applicable
7. If necessary, tell them you'll be right with them	Applicable	Not applicable
8. Invite them to sit next to you	Applicable	Not applicable
9. Use their name	Applicable	Not applicable
10. Use the word *you*	Applicable	Not applicable
11. Echo their words, mirror their mood	Applicable	Not applicable
12. Cultivate a neat, professional appearance and environment	Applicable	Not applicable

Which apply? You probably decided that all of them do. This should reinforce an overriding concept: *Sales and service skills are critical at all levels of business and in all four forms of selling:* front-line-to-the-public, business-to-business, within-business and, in certain ways, nonpersonal selling.

GREAT PHONE WELCOMES

Selling by phone is a challenging task. All those visual clues that support in-person selling disappear. Yet it's surprising how many of the very same strategies of face-to-face selling apply even to phone sales.

Return to that list of twelve welcoming tactics you learned earlier. Which ones *don't* apply to telephone sales? Write their numbers here:

In all probability, you listed the following: 1, 2, 3, 5, 8, and 12. Two of these may require some rethinking.

#5—smiling—applies to phone greetings more than you'd think. In fact, most experts agree that you can actually sense a smile over the phone. If the seller's greeting sounds bored, unfriendly, mechanical, or disinterested, that greeting will undermine all that will follow.

#12 may be relevant, too. Environmental sounds in the background during a phone conversation can be even more distracting than when they occur during an in-person sale.

All the other techniques . . .

- Using a natural greeting phrase
- Thinking of your customer as an old friend
- Telling them you'll be right with them (if you must put them on hold)
- Using the client's name (just after the greeting, if you've determined that name; e.g., "Yes, Mr. Smith, I'll be glad to help you.")
- Using the word *you*
- Echoing their words, mirroring their mood

. . . take on even greater significance in a phone welcome. The reason: You have far fewer strategies at your disposal.

The Phone Welcome Formula

You've probably heard phone greetings hundreds of times. Think about how they're usually phrased. Picture that you work at Acme Travel. You've answered the phone. Write the greeting you'd give here:

Is your greeting composed of two or three words? Not a good idea. For example, "Acme Travel," in and of itself, might be efficient, but it would also be soulless. Did you give your name? Great. Research shows that if you volunteer your name in your welcome, the likelihood that the caller will feel comfortable about giving his or her name will be much higher. Did you remember what you read earlier about asking an open-ended question (like "How may I help you?" rather than "May I help you?")? If you did, then you no doubt incorporated it into your example.

According to researchers, here's the perfect greeting:

- "Good morning (or afternoon or evening)
- (Your company's or division's name)
- This is (your name)
- How may I help you?"

This greeting has every element of the perfect welcome. It starts with a positive emotion, identifies the company, offers your name, and invites the caller to an exploration of how you might assist him.

It does seem rather long, though. And it will *feel* long after you've said it hundreds of times. *But that length is necessary:* It takes several seconds for the caller's mind to really "connect" with the exchange that's about to begin. The four-part greeting allows time for that to happen.

Your greeting should not sound "automatic." It may be the 46th time you've used it today, but it's the first time your caller has heard it from you. You should sound reasonably excited as you welcome them. After all, the person is about to take a trip—probably a vacation—and is excited about it. You must mirror this back from the very start. Even business travelers need to hear enthusiasm in your voice. They, too, hope their trip will be a positive one and, perhaps, a little bit exciting.

In Chapter 7 we'll return, in greater depth, to how to maximize your overall telephone sales and service skills.

WELCOMES IN OTHER MEDIA

Is the welcome a factor in situations other than phone or face-to-face selling? Does it work in nonpersonal circumstances? Absolutely.

Here's proof. If it's convenient for you now, log onto the Internet. Go to a Web site that's travel-related, like Expedia or Travelocity. How does the *first page* you see make you feel? Describe that feeling below. (If it's not convenient, try to remember one home page you're especially familiar with.) Also, try to account for the reasons *why* you felt the way you did when that first page popped on the screen.

A Web site's home page is its "welcome." What makes it friendly? Colors, on-screen phrases, the apparent simplicity of navigation, photos and, possibly, sound effects conspire to create an initial impression. Travel Web sites especially need to generate a quick sense of fun, excitement, and efficiency, because that's what is being promised.

The same applies to sales communication via e-mail. The very first sentence the e-mailer uses sets the tone for all to come. And what of other sell pieces? The first image of a TV commercial, the first thing your eye is drawn to in a newspaper ad, and the first words you hear in a radio commercial serve as "virtual" welcomes. Indeed, when ad designers create a company's message, they may spend hours, even days, thinking and rethinking the elements that create the first, enduring, welcoming impression.

DETERMINING NEEDS

Consider this situation. You meet someone from out of town. She tells you, "I don't know your city very well. Where should I have dinner tomorrow night?" What would you recommend (in your own city or town)? Write it here:

Did you actually give a recommendation? If you did, *how could you know what this person will like?* A steakhouse? What if she's a vegetarian? In other words, you should have first written: "I'd ask her some questions to find out what she might like." And that leads to our next major topic: determining needs.

You've welcomed your customer warmly, enthusiastically, and with genuine interest. It's now time to guide that customer in a discovery of what he wants and needs through efficient interviewing (also known as qualifying). But you'll have to adjust, according to the situation. Keep these three preliminary factors in mind:

Is This Someone You Know?

If you do, you should build on the information and relationship you already have. (That's why it's great, if it's feasible in your selling situation, to keep a file on a client and refer to it beforehand.) Maybe this is one of hundreds, even thousands, of customers you deal with. But you may be the only travel professional this client knows, at least the only one she will deal with that day.

If you don't know the customer, you must build a relationship from scratch. Make that great first impression, then move on quickly to an exploration of his or her needs.

CAN SERVICEPEOPLE "KNOW" CUSTOMERS?

Indeed they can. For example, Marriott International keeps a database on all the customers who stay at its hotels, across almost all of its dozen brands. An alert front-desk clerk at, say, the Renaissance Hotel in Beverly Hills will know that this guest stayed at the Ritz-Carlton in Atlanta and that the guest prefers firm pillows. To acknowledge that information at check-in and to offer to do something about it will establish an instant friendship between the guest and the front-desk professional.

Is This Someone Who Knows What He Wants?

Several surveys have concluded that four distinct kinds of buyers exist. Each type of buyer possesses a different depth of knowledge. Your approach should be tailored to that level of knowledge.

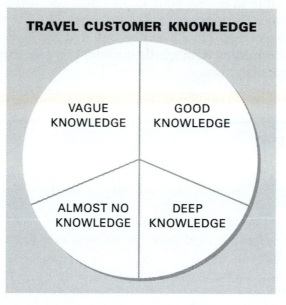

TRAVEL CUSTOMER KNOWLEDGE

VAGUE KNOWLEDGE

GOOD KNOWLEDGE

ALMOST NO KNOWLEDGE

DEEP KNOWLEDGE

If a customer seems to know exactly what he wants, don't automatically apply transactional selling. That would be a big mistake. You should spend a little time exploring what the client's beliefs are based on. Friends? The media? Internet research? Personal experience? The answers you get will provide significant clues as to what you should do next. Remember: The customer isn't the expert. You are. Otherwise, he probably wouldn't have contacted you. (Some extremely well-informed consumers, however, do go to professionals. The usual reason: to save time.)

Exploring levels of knowledge is most appropriate to sellers who are clearly consultative, like travel agents. However, other travel professionals can benefit from assessing a client's understanding of the travel experience. Let's review some examples that prove it.

Here is a series of assumptions that a reasonably well-informed customer might have. Each addresses a different sector of the travel industry. Circle *True* or *False*, based on your own knowledge.

1. A direct flight and a nonstop flight are the same thing.   True   False
2. Adjoining rooms in a hotel have a door between them.   True   False
3. If you're on a "hosted" tour, a tour manager will take care of your needs.   True   False
4. Hawaii is rainiest in the summer.   True   False
5. An intermediate car is usually the same as a mid-size car.   True   False

6. A cruise ship's inside staterooms don't have windows.   True   False
7. Airplanes take people faster from city to city than trains do.   True   False
8. Car rentals always cost more if you pick up in one city and drop off in another.   True   False

Time to assess your knowledge: All of the statements are false, except #5 (see the sidebar for the reasons). The point: Even knowledgeable consumers may have assumptions that are erroneous. Unless you test these assumptions with gentle questioning, you may have a very unhappy customer later on.

WHY ARE THEY FALSE?

1. A non-stop flight doesn't make any stops between a passenger's departure and destination cities, but a direct flight stops in at least one city along the way. There's just no change of planes.
2. *Connecting* rooms have a door between them.
3. There's no tour manager on a hosted tour. (An *escorted* tour has a tour manager.)
4. Winters are rainier in Hawaii.
5. This one's true!
6. Some inside staterooms do have windows. For example, Royal Caribbean's Voyager-class vessels have inside staterooms with windows that open on interior atrium shopping areas.
7. High-speed trains often carry people faster from the center of one city to another, especially when you consider such air factors as taking a taxi to the airport, waiting in line at check-in, etc.
8. Sometimes "drop-off" fees are charged, sometimes not. It depends on the car rental firm and the destination.

And what of people who know almost nothing, or those who know a lot, but don't know what they want? That's good news for sellers of travel, even though such a client may require more time and attention. These customers are placing their travel future into your hands. They trust you to find the best solution for them. What more could you ask for?

Is the Customer a Shopper, a Browser, or a Buyer?

These terms come up all the time in certain retail environments, like furniture stores, clothing boutiques, and computer stores. They're rarely used in travel. That's unfortunate, because they're highly useful.

Shoppers   Let's start with travel shoppers. Consider the following scenarios:

- A person asks an airline reservationist the price of a flight from Seattle to Seoul on April 16.
- Someone inquires of a car reservationist what a full-size car, with unlimited mileage, will cost if he picks it up from Logan Airport on June 10 and drops off at La Guardia on June 17.

• A person asks a travel agent the price of a Holland America Inside Passage cruise to Alaska, departing August 29, for a stateroom in F Category.

Now give at least three things you can conclude about what each of these shoppers might have in common:

1.

2.

3.

Compare your answers to the following. A travel shopper:

1. Usually uses the **telephone** (in these cases) or the **Internet**
2. Has already done **a lot of research**
3. Will make the same **inquiry to multiple sources** (e.g., four car rental firms)
4. Is **unwilling to give personal information**, at least initially
5. Is looking for the **best deal** and is committed almost exclusively to **price**

What should your goal be with a shopper? To make your company "the last stop." How is that done? Here are five strategies to deal with shoppers:

1. **Offer to make a reservation without requiring any immediate financial commitment.** This classic approach, used by almost all segments of the industry, presumes a partial commitment is better than none and increases the likelihood that the caller will book with you. Shoppers often resist this, however, knowing that everyone they call will do the same.

2. **Use a fear-based closing tactic.** These tactics are recognizably manipulative, but many companies swear by them. Some examples: "This rate may not be available later." "These staterooms are selling fast."

3. **Muddy the waters.** As long as a shopper is comparing apples to apples, price comparisons are easy. With apples and oranges, it's a lot harder. The "muddy the waters" strategy requires you to introduce alternatives to the shopper that he or she may not have considered. For example, if you were a travel agent and someone called about airfare to Europe, you might counter with a tour or cruise that includes airfare, stressing the value that the package represents.

4. **Ask the shopper to call back to see if you can match the best price he received.** If you turn out to be the most pleasant and helpful person he talked to, the shopper might very well come back to you to see if you can match the lowest price he was quoted. The danger: He may try to trick you with a false, impossible-to-match price, one you can only offer if most of your profit evaporates. (This, of course, doesn't usually apply to reservationists, because it's hard for a caller to recontact a person among hundreds.)

5. **Ask qualifying questions.** This may be the best tactic of all. Instead of quoting a price immediately, ask a few "explorer" questions. This gets the buyer off the "shopper" track and positions you as perhaps the only person who cared. Even if the shopper gathers prices from others, you'll stand out and be the person she will call back to handle her business.

Browsers   Browsers can be far more frustrating than shoppers. In many ways, they're the *opposite* of shoppers. Very willing to divulge personal information to you, they want plenty of attention, take up a lot of your time, have little product knowledge, don't know what they want and aren't serious about their trip—yet, or ever.

Through careful but limited questioning, you must swiftly determine if the person just isn't yet focused and might simply need your help to become a buyer, now or later. However, if you discover that he's just a "dreamer" who'll never really buy travel from you or anyone, and is just killing time (yours and his), you probably have to politely wrap up the conversation and move on to a real prospect.

Buyers   Buyers are ideal customers. They definitely want to *book travel* and place their trust in you. They may have once been browsers or shoppers, but you impressed them with your skills and clear-cut commitment to satisfy them. The best way to demonstrate that is by careful questioning to determine their needs.

In a way, a salesperson—especially a consultative one like a travel agent—interviews a client in much the same way that a talk show host does. Think of one you've watched, like Larry King, Ted Koppel, or Oprah. Write down what you think are their three biggest secrets to their success.

The host you chose: _____

The three secrets to his or her success:

1.

2.

3.

Now here are the three "secrets" to his success that Larry King gave in a *People Magazine* article:

- "I keep my questions brief."
- "I listen carefully to the guest's answers."
- "I leave myself as much out of the conversation as possible."

INTERVIEWING AND MARKET ANALYSIS

Interviewing tactics that salespeople use are very similar to those that are used in marketing studies. Their purpose is the same, too: to assess a marketplace's needs, then tailor promotions to those consumer needs.

GREAT CLIENT INTERVIEWING: THE SECRETS

The very same strategies that Larry King uses are hugely valuable when determining a customer's needs. Let's add them to a list of "Seven Secrets to Great Client Interviewing." Though they're especially relevant to travel agents, many of them are valuable to supplier reservationists, hotel concierges, and business-to-business sellers, too.

Secret #1: Lead with Chitchat

Numerous studies have shown that when the seller and buyer initially talk about *anything* other than what the client is about to buy, the likelihood of a purchase dramatically increases. Face-to-face selling, however, is the only situation where this is easily done. This small talk must be kept brief, however. Otherwise the time-profit ratio will be unacceptable.

Secret #2: Get the Vanguard Questions Out of the Way

Often called closed-ended questions, **vanguard questions elicit short, simple, factual answers from the client.** They usually occur after the welcome or the chitchat. Vanguard questions force the client to focus, allow the seller to keep control of the process and clarify, early on, whether the customer is a buyer, browser, or shopper. The vanguard questions most relevant to travel are:

- **Who** will be going?
- **What** do you have in mind? (An independent trip? A tour? A cruise? A business trip? First class?)
- **Where** do you intend to go?
- **When** do you want to go?
- **How long** will you be staying?
- **How much** have you set aside for the trip?

In some cases (e.g., for travel agents), the seller must get responses to *all* of these questions before proceeding. In other cases, the salesperson needs to ask only selected ones or slightly adjust for the sales situation. For instance, an airline or hotel reservationist will ask all of these questions, except the "how much" one. Instead, she will simply give the price of the requested flight or hotel room. (This is true for most transactional and commodity-driven sales situations.)

In some cases it's a good idea to *support* the question. "So I can find the best value for you, give me an idea of how much you've set aside for your trip" explains *why* you've posed your question. It describes the benefit of your query.

The phrasing of each question can also vary according to the context. For example, a business-to-business salesperson may say, "Tell me a little about your budget range." This wording is better, because it tends to prevent the client from citing a simple, often unrealistic price. Experienced salespeople also usually assume, with good reason, that the *real* price the client is willing to pay is a bit higher than the top number in the range given.

Finally, vanguard questions can sometimes lead to follow-up queries. A budget-range question may lead to "Are you flexible with your travel dates, just in case I can get you a better value?" Or "What do you have in mind?" may lead to "Are you celebrating a special occasion?"

Secret #3: Use Explorer Questions

Explorer questions uncover your customers' attitudes, perceptions, feelings, and concerns. Often called open-ended questions, explorer questions elicit much more detailed, analytical answers than the factual vanguard ones do. They provide a glimpse into the deeper, more complex needs that a client may have. A cornerstone of consultative selling, they're essential to selling travel experiences, like cruises, tours and complicated trips, as well as to help people who don't precisely know what they want arrive at a decision.

ARE THERE ANY QUESTIONS?

You would think that most travel agents ask plenty of questions of their clients. This CLIA study suggests otherwise. Percentage of travel agents who . . .

- Asked client's name: 36%
- Asked about previous vacations: 23%
- Asked about preferred activities: 29%

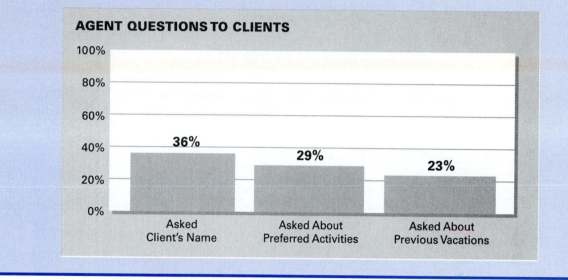

AGENT QUESTIONS TO CLIENTS

Some examples:

- "Give me an idea of what kind of trip you had in mind."
- "What are you looking for the most from your vacation?"
- "If you had three goals for this trip, what would they be?"
- "What do you expect to do during your vacation?"
- "What makes you want to visit this place?"
- "What kind of hotels do you usually stay in?"
- "What did you enjoy the most on your last vacation?"
- "What was your favorite vacation ever, and why?"
- "What was your least favorite vacation ever, and why?"
- "How much socializing do you like to do while on vacation?"

Typically, explorer questions are applicable to major travel purchase decisions (e.g., buying a two-week vacation package). But they're relevant to "smaller" situations, too. For instance, a guest might approach a hotel concierge about which city tour to take. Rather than recommend a generic, all-purpose tour, the concierge might briefly explore the guest's likes and dislikes. This could lead to a recommendation of a more specialized or extended tour, one that might better satisfy the guest's special interests.

Reminders About Explorer Questions   What else should you know about explorer questions? Here are five thoughts:

- The less sure a customer is about what he or she wants, the more explorer questions you'll need to ask.
- You also should use a few explorer questions with customers who seem to know exactly what they want. The reason: They may, in reality, know less than they think. At the very least, it will set you apart as an interested and caring salesperson—something, as you've learned, that works especially well with shoppers.
- Avoid getting too personal with your questions, especially early on. It may make your client uneasy.
- You should be prepared to extend an explorer question with a follow-up one. For instance, if a person says she usually stays at Four Seasons or Ritz-Carlton hotels, you should delve into the reasons why she favors those chains. The subsequent response may lead you directly to what kind of trip components you should recommend.
- When exploring a customer's needs, be sensitive to his time constraints (and yours). Qualifying your client should be an efficient, tight process, one that doesn't monopolize a client's time for too long or drain your own schedule of valuable time.

Now that you know a little more about explorer questions, try the following. Come up with three more explorer questions you might add to our list:

1.

Four Seasons hotels are very attractive to upscale travelers. *(Photo by Marc Mancini)*

2.

3.

LIFESTYLE QUESTIONS

When a travel salesperson asks questions that are not directly involved with travel but that do **probe the values that a client holds,** he's asking **lifestyle questions.** (Lifestyle questions are also critical to those who conduct marketing studies.) These lifestyle questions can be either vanguard questions or explorer questions. Some examples:

- What kind of car do you drive?
- What are your two favorite TV shows? Why?
- Which magazines do you subscribe to?
- Do you have a hobby? What is it?
- How do you spend your spare time?

The answers to questions like these often provide useful insights into what pleases a client, and what doesn't. For example, someone who favors shows on the Discovery Channel might be interested in a culture/enrichment tour. A person whose hobby is parasailing might be ready for Oahu's East Shore. Someone who drives a Honda Civic is probably thrifty and likes things simple. A modest, economical trip, perhaps with lodging at a Fairfield, Hampton, or Days Inn, will probably please that client.

Carefully phrase your lifestyle questions, though. Otherwise they may seem intrusive. A good idea: Preface them with "I'm going to ask you a few questions about your lifestyle. It's just to get a few clues to your needs."

Secret #4: Ask Three Questions for Every One Statement You Make

Good salespeople leave themselves out of the picture. They don't talk about their preferences, only those of their clients. In fact, good salespeople *cringe* when a client asks, "Well, what do *you* like?" It's not about what the seller likes, but what *the customer will like*. "It's about what *you* like . . ." should be the salesperson's answer to that dreaded question and a springboard to good qualifying. Doing this also helps prevent a form of selling that works poorly in the travel industry: qualifying by presentation. Rather than asking questions and fulfilling needs, the salesperson who qualifies by presentation rattles off a series of facts about the product. You may even have seen this kind of sales presentation in a store or on TV:

It slices! It dices! It has 17 functions in one tool. And there's more!

The equivalent in travel:

This hotel has a swimming pool, great views (etc.), while this one has (etc.) and this one has (etc.)

This sort of "data dumping" has no place in consultative selling, nor does it work very well with transactional selling, either.

So, if you make an effort to pose more questions than you answer—three times more, in fact—you can't help but remain focused on the client and avoid qualifying by presentation.

Secret #5: Use Contrasting Questions

A contrasting question is an either/or query:

- "Do you want to kick back or to be really active on this vacation?"
- "Are you looking for a familiar or an exotic experience?"
- "Is your ideal vacation a cultural exploration or for just having fun?"

Contrasting questions lie somewhere between vanguard and explorer questions. They also require customers to put themselves at a point along a sort of scale. Take that last example. The answer might be: "I want to go to Cancun mostly to have some fun, but I wouldn't mind a day trip to some archaeological site." Or "I want to use Cancun only as a base to go out to see the ruins at Chichen Itza, Uxmal, and Tulum." As you can see, we have two people going to the same place, but on very different points of the contrasting question scale.

A COMPUTER WANTS TO KNOW

Travel Web sites usually pose only vanguard questions. Some use contrasting questions, requesting that you place your cursor on a point on a scale. A few make limited use of explorer questions by giving you multiple-choice answers from which to choose. The ability to deal with explorer questions, however, has eluded computer programmers, since the answers are so open-ended and unpredictable.

Secret #6: Be Alert to Hot-Button Answers

A **hot button is something the client seems especially passionate about.** For example, if you were a hotel reservationist and mentioned that the rooms at your hotel were extra spacious, the potential guest might sound particularly excited and interested. The reason: She's bringing her two children and knows that ample space is a real plus. Indeed, for most families, spaciousness is a significant hot button.

Pay close attention to your customer's responses. If she gets suddenly excited, whatever ignited that excitement should be more fully explored and later incorporated into your recommendation.

Secret #7: Stay Alert

Did you ever read a book and suddenly realize that you've read several pages *without being aware of anything you've just read?* Strange, isn't it?

Alertness levels vary from minute to minute, even second to second. But as a salesperson, it's vital that you remain vigilant for your customers' responses and even to their nonverbal cues.

Let's see how good a listener you are. Answer each question by circling the number that applies. At the end, count up your point total.

Question	Never	Occasionally	Often	Usually	Always
1. When I am listening to someone, do I pay attention, rather than fake it?	1	2	3	4	5
2. While listening, do I pick up on the feelings and attitudes of the speaker, as well as the mere words?	1	2	3	4	5
3. Do I block out distractions when listening to somebody?	1	2	3	4	5
4. Do I manage to avoid letting my own attitudes block out what is being said, if I disagree with the person?	1	2	3	4	5
5. Do I pick up on nonverbal cues that may communicate what the person is saying over and above his/her words?	1	2	3	4	5
6. Do I manage to avoid interrupting the person talking?	1	2	3	4	5
7. Do I succeed in paying attention to slow, rambling, or boring individuals?	1	2	3	4	5
8. Do I refrain from thinking up what I'm going to say to someone before they're finished talking?	1	2	3	4	5
9. Do I keep eye contact with the person who's talking to me?	1	2	3	4	5
10. When the person is done talking, do I verbally indicate that I have understood (or not understood) what they have said?	1	2	3	4	5

Your total score: _____

Scoring:

40–50 = You're an extremely alert listener

35–39 = You're a good listener

25–34 = You pay attention but perhaps should work on your listening skills

Under 25 = You must work on your listening skills

How to Be a Better Listener

The key to good listening is this: Listening is an *active* skill, not a passive one. To keep your listening active, follow the ALERT formula:

Avoid going on tangents

Look at your client (in-person) or imagine them (on phone)

Exclude your personal feelings

Reduce distractions

Take notes

Do this, and you'll *listen* your customers into buying.

SO WHY SO MUCH ABOUT TRAVEL AGENTS?

We refer to travel agents a lot in this chapter and elsewhere. Why? Perhaps you want to be a travel agent! But also, the strategies that agents use to sell consultatively apply to many other jobs in travel. Finally, no matter what sector of travel you're in, you must understand how travel agents work. The reason: Travel agencies still account for the majority of travel sales, perhaps even of the products you represent. Travel agents still sell 60 percent of all flights, despite the fact that the airlines have done all they can to steer business away from agencies and directly to their Web sites and reservation lines. Travel agents remain a lynchpin of the travel business.

PROSPECTING

In most of the sales situations you've read about, the buyer takes the initial steps: He may call, visit, go on the Internet or happen to read an ad.

But in some businesses, **salespeople take the first step and actively seek out potential buyers.** This is called **prospecting.** Three examples: an office supplies salesperson visits a series of businesses in one large office building, asking to speak to each company's purchasing agent; a representative from a phone service company (e.g., AT&T) calls people at home to offer a new, competitive calling plan; a real estate broker attends a Rotary Club meeting, with the primary purpose of finding out—casually, of course—if any of the attendees may be in the market to buy a home.

Can you think of any situations where *you* were prospected by a business or organization? Write two examples here:

1.

2.

Prospecting can take two forms: direct and indirect. **Direct prospecting involves contacting the potential buyer with the intention of making the sales pitch, then and there.** Direct prospecting can be *random* (like the office supplies salesperson going door-to-door) or *prequalified* (as with the phone service representative, who works from a database list of households that fit a predetermined profile of individuals who might be open to changing their phone service providers). Of course, direct prospecting is rarely entirely random. That seller of office supplies went into a building knowing—perhaps from the lobby directory—that the companies inside were the kind who buy a lot of office supplies.

Indirect prospecting, on the other hand, involves putting yourself in a situation where the opportunity to sell *may* occur. Parties, conferences, social gatherings, even lunch with a friend could lead to a sale. Good salespeople are always alert to sales opportunities, even if they're somewhere for a purpose other than selling. That clerk at the video store you regularly go to may desperately need a vacation. And you're ready to sell her one.

A few other thoughts on prospecting:

- **Prospecting requires many, if not all, of the same sales steps you've learned in this book.** You must greet the person warmly, determine needs, recommend solutions, address concerns, enhance the sale, achieve an agreement, and follow up.
- A **cold prospect** is one you approach without the buyer expecting your sales effort. Doing so—whether in person, on the phone or otherwise—is called a *cold call*. Our two first examples (office supplies and phone service) were both cold calls.

SECRETS OF COLD CALLING

Cold call prospecting is a fiercely challenging form of sales. Here, in brief, are some of the "secrets" that most expert cold callers know:

- Know your objective(s) in advance.
- Be friendly, polite, courteous, and warm from the very start.
- Try to find out the name of the purchase decision-maker in advance. Ask for that person.
- Be especially friendly to the "gatekeeper" (e.g., receptionist) who acts as a "screen" between you and the buyer.
- Explain your purpose up front.
- Be slightly tentative. Overslick or overconfident doesn't work.
- Refer to other current customers, if you can.
- Listen attentively; don't try to take over.
- Time your calls to early morning or just before lunch, when gatekeepers may not be around to deflect your call.
- On calls, never sound like you're reading from a script.
- Have a strong ego and don't take rejection personally.

- One form of prospecting that has become popular is *asking satisfied customers for referrals*. Referral business is extremely productive. A study from Orlando's Bill Bishop and Associates discovered that 60 percent to 80 percent of referred leads buy. (**A lead is someone you find out about who may be interested in buying products like yours.**) They buy an average of 23 percent more than "regular" customers do.
- Prospecting—especially when the prospect shows interest and consultative selling is involved—often *leads to a scheduled appointment*. At that time, the sales cycle will more fully unfold.

Prospecting in the Travel Industry

Front-line-to-the-public prospecting is not a major sales avenue in the travel industry, except in certain segments (e.g., timeshare lodging). It occurs regularly, however, in business-to-business situations. Two examples:

- A hotel sales director, in the hope of capturing their business, calls tour operators whose tours visit his area.
- A cruise line executive attends a "Cruisathon" convention, where she convinces the owner of a medium-size travel agency chain to sell more of her product.

SUMMING UP SALES

Imagine this. You go to a doctor with a complaint that you've been having headaches. You suggest to the doctor that you suspect you also have high blood pressure—this must be the cause of the headaches—so could he fill out a prescription for Cardizem for you? He says "sure," efficiently fills out the prescription and sends you on your way.

What's wrong with this scenario? Explain briefly here:

You probably wrote that you couldn't possibly have known what the exact cause of the problem was. Moreover, the doctor should have asked you some questions, done some tests and certainly not automatically gone along with the drug you asked for.

Yet travel salespeople often fail to ask questions, simply agree with their clients, and just give the traveler what he asks for. If a physician gives a prescription without a diagnosis, it's malpractice. If a travel salesperson gives advice without a "diagnosis," it's just plain unprofessional.

To connect with your travel customers, you must, in a warm, friendly, and caring manner, explore what's best for them. Then you'll be truly ready to make the perfect recommendation, the subject of our next chapter.

Name: _____   Date: _____

ACTIVITY #1   WATCH AND LEARN

Go to a restaurant—either full-service or fast-food—and sit at a strategic table (one where you can observe the employees). Watch the behavior of these people. How good is each, based on the things you learned in this chapter? (Some concepts that apply to travel may not be relevant to the dining industry.) Then fill out the following:

Important note: You should be as subtle and unobtrusive about this exercise as possible. If anyone asks what you're doing, explain that it's part of a class you're taking.

1. How are customers greeted? (For a full-service restaurant: at the entrance; at a fast-food place: at the food service counter.) Describe what you observe.

2. Have you noticed one person who is doing his or her job especially well? What is it about that person that makes him or her so effective?

3. Have you noticed one person who is *not* doing his or her job very well? What made you conclude this?

4. Does the restaurant have any positive "atmospheres" that helps customers feel good about their experience? Any negative ones?

Name: _____ Date: _____

ACTIVITY #2   EXPLORE YOUR WANTS

Below are some of the sample explorer questions we cited in this chapter. It's time for *you* to answer them. Project your thoughts to your next major vacation and respond to each. Put your answers in the space provided. Try to keep your thoughts vague. *(Don't focus on a destination yet.)*

1. What kind of hotels do you usually stay in?

2. What did you enjoy the most on your last vacation?

3. What was your favorite vacation ever, and why?

4. What was your least favorite vacation ever, and why?

5. What kind of trip do you have in mind for your next vacation?

6. What are you looking for the most from your vacation?

7. What do you expect to do during your vacation?

Now go back to the dream vacation you described in Chapter 1. Does it fit the answers you gave to these seven questions? Why or why not?

Name: _____   Date: _____

ACTIVITY #3   WHAT DO FRIENDS WANT?

Ask a friend the very same questions that you were asked in Activity 2. Explain that they should keep their mind open to anything—no particular place or experiences should dominate their thinking for now. In fact, they should mention no destination at all to you while you determine their needs and make a recommendation. Put their answers in the spaces provided.

Who is the friend: _____

1. What kind of hotels do you usually stay in?

2. What did you enjoy the most on your last vacation?

3. What was your favorite vacation ever, and why?

4. What was your least favorite vacation ever, and why?

5. What kind of trip do you have in mind for your next vacation?

6. What are you looking for the most from your vacation?

7. What do you expect to do during your vacation?

Now, if you can, guess the kind of trip and place you think your friend would like, based on his or her answers. Write it here:

Tell him or her your idea. How does your friend react?

Are your friend's answers to the seven questions very different from the ones you gave in Activity 2? Why or why not?

3
Recommending Solutions and Addressing Concerns

OBJECTIVES

After reading this chapter, you'll be able to:

- Conduct efficient research

- Apply the eight rules of recommending

- Interpret exclusive and preferred supplier relationships

- Deliver effective sales presentations

- Address customer concerns

If you're a woman, read the left-hand column below this sentence. If you're a man, read the right-hand column.

It was the best dress you ever bought.
You had been looking and looking. Nothing grabbed your attention. You visited your sixth shop, the seventh, the eighth. Ready to give up, you halfheartedly walked

It was the best suit you ever bought. Not that you buy suits very often. You're a casual kind of guy. But even a casual guy needs one great suit.
You had been looking and looking. Nothing grabbed your attention. You visited

into one more store. It *did* look promising.

The sales clerk was gracious and warm. She asked what you wanted to look at, what size dress you wore, what it was for. More questions, too.

She disappeared into the back and returned with the perfect dress. It looked right, felt right, fit right, even though it wasn't exactly what you had in mind.

No matter. You loved it. You bought it.

Did it challenge your budget a bit? Sure. But so what? It was perfect.

one store, another, another. This was taking too long. You *hate* shopping.

One more store. The sales clerk was gracious and knowledgeable. He asked what you needed it for, what color you were thinking of, all sorts of questions.

He led you to a rack and pulled out a suit. This was it. It looked right, felt right, you tried it on and it fit perfectly. This was *your* suit.

No, it didn't exactly match what you had in mind. No matter. You bought it.

Was it more than you had expected to pay? Sure. But so what? It was perfect.

Buying a vacation isn't all that different from buying clothing. With travel, you wonder where you should go, what you should pay, arrive at a vague notion about what it should be, then find the right professional to help you do it.

That travel professional asks you questions, determines your needs and makes one, *maybe* two recommendations. Her goal: that the recommendation fits your personality. It doesn't matter that her proposed travel solution doesn't exactly match what you had in mind. If it seems right, maybe perfect, you'll ask her to book it, even though it may be a bit more than you expected to spend.

The key, of course, is that a good salesperson in any field takes the responses you give to well-framed questions and suggests something that fits your needs. Clothes, cars, skateboards, cell phones—it doesn't matter, the same principles are at work.

There is one difference, though. Travel is more complicated than most products, even when it's primarily a commodity. Quite often you have to do research before you make your recommendation.

Before reading further, though, write below two specific sources you usually consult when you research your own travel:

1.

2.

Now write down the reasons you go to these sources:

1.

2.

RESEARCHING TRAVEL

Usually, travel professionals conduct two kinds of research before they can recommend something and ask for the customer's business. What they do is not unlike what a consumer does before making a vacation choice:

1. Transactional Research

Transactional research is a simple matter of responding to a customer's logistic and price needs—discovered through vanguard questions—**with the particulars of what the salesperson sells**. Such research is usually required for selling both travel commodities and experiences, and is carried out by both transactional and consultative salespeople. It's almost always done on computer systems. It's essential to efficient front-line-to-the-public service and selling. Some examples:

- A travel agent or airline reservationist consults a computer system to see if a round-trip flight to San Francisco is available for the days, times, and price that the customer prefers.

- A cruise line reservationist checks stateroom availability for a travel agent who has called on behalf of his clients.
- A person at a car rental desk checks to see if there are any full-size autos left—she suggests an upgrade from mid-size for only $3 more a day and the customer agrees.

Transactional research usually takes place during the conversation between the potential buyer and the sales- or serviceperson. Occasionally it's done after the fact, with the salesperson contacting the client once the research is completed.

2.   Consultative Research

Consultative research may require more time than does the transactional kind, **since you're trying to address a client's deeper and more complex travel needs.** It depends on the situation. If a client wants a travel agent to plan a fifteen-day trip through Europe, staying in four cities (hotel research will be needed), with air and a car rental involved, the agent will—after determining what kind of trip he wants—be obliged to do the following:

- **Transactionally:** Check airfares, car-rental rates and hotel costs, usually on her **CRS (Computer Reservation System),** which other segments of the industry usually call the **GDS (Global Distribution System).** Increasingly, such transactional research can also be done on the Internet.
- **Consultatively:** Use **trade resources** (sources usually available to travel professionals only) and **consumer resources** (sources the public can access) to research those destinations and hotels she isn't already familiar with. These resources may be computer- or print-based.

All this, of course, will take time. Many travel agents charge a fee for planning out a complicated, "a la carte," component-by-component type of trip. (The industry calls these **FITs,** though no one really agrees on what those letters stand for.)

The travel counselor may also suggest something entirely different to replace the FIT, like a cruise or a tour, which could be booked on the spot through her CRS, the Internet or with one phone call.

Travel agents aren't the only industry professionals who do consultative research. Those working in any of our four sales models (front-line-to-the-public, business-to-business, within-business, and nonpersonal sales) almost always carry out research and find solutions before they can sell their ideas, services, or products.

THE SEVEN SECRET SOURCES

Certain valuable resources seem not to be as well known to travel professionals as they should be. Here are seven of them, with descriptions:

- **The Weissmann Travel Reports.** Information on virtually every destination in the world, both well known and obscure. Weissmann gives sample itineraries, food and shopping tips, "Do's and Don't's," plus all the basics. Available via on-line subscription.
- **Nationwide Intelligence.** This company publishes several valuable insider information resources. Its *Travel Alert Bulletin* (26 issues yearly) provides news flashes on potential airline, airport, and destination opportunities and problems. The *Personal Travel Report* (monthly) rates the best values in hotels, airlines, etc., provides insider tips/alerts and profiles a key business city in each issue (with airport profiles). And the *Airline, Airport*, and *City Briefings* provide reports on principal U.S. airlines, cities, and airports (including all manner of statistics, phone numbers, etc.).
- **The Consumer Reports Travel Letter.** Consumer Reports brings its assess-all approach to our industry in this monthly publication. Very valuable, unique topics are covered, including frequent-flyer programs, airline seat pitch, upgrade strategies, airline lounge clubs, travel insurance, consolidators, airline and hotel ratings, etc. Considerable leisure and business travel information.
- **CultureGrams.** The source of cultural information on over 100 countries. Information on greetings, dining, dress, food, business hours, body language and the like. Great to prepare international business travelers.
- **World Travel Guide.** This single-volume reference work gives enormous detail—including information for business travel— about virtually every nation on earth. Its slick, professional presentation—with generous use of color—is impressive. Plenty on climate, nightlife, history, food, drink, and sports. Also available in CD-ROM format and on-line.
- **World Weather Guide.** From Afghanistan to Zimbabwe, *WWG* is a comprehensive guide to the weather in every country for every month of the year. It includes over 450 charts and maps, and is excellent for business or leisure travelers. Detailed information—temperature, humidity, comfort index, climate changes, rainfall, wind-chill index and geography—is provided for over 500 cities.
- **The Star Service.** This huge, unbiased volume critiques thousands of hotels worldwide and sometimes even cites where the better rooms (size, views, etc.) in each are located. Also available on-line.

The World Travel Guide is a rich source of destination information. *(Courtesy of Travelknowledge.com)*

RECOMMENDING SOLUTIONS

In purely transactional situations, the recommendation is usually a matter-of-fact, logistic one. Say it's a question of finding the best price for a flight between Los Angeles and Bermuda.

Your CRS tells you that there's no nonstop or direct flight between the two destinations. A connection will be necessary, possibly with an overnight stopover at a hotel between flights, you inform the client. The most obvious choice: Delta from LAX to Atlanta, then the next day Atlanta to Bermuda on Delta.

So does *no* creative thinking go into this solution at all? Not necessarily. You remember learning in travel school that often the shortest distance on a long west-east flight is a routing that curves toward the pole. You research more deeply into your CRS and discover you could route the customer on Air Canada, connecting in Toronto (instead of Atlanta). The price would be the same, but the flight time would be forty-five minutes shorter! Moreover, when you tell the client of your idea, he says he's always wanted to visit Toronto, even for a brief overnight. Your solution is far better than the obvious one. Yes, even in a transactional sale you can bring something extra, a solution that goes beyond mere order-taking service.

The Rules of Recommending

Consultative selling, however, does usually demand more thought, insight, and skill than transactional selling does. Sales experts have come up with a raft of recommendation strategies to maximize your selling success (some of which apply to transactional selling, too). Let's call them the Eight Rules of Recommending.

Rule #1: Recap the Customer's Needs   Have you noticed that when you go to a McDonald's drive-through, the order-taker repeats what you requested? Some McDonald's locations even have a small screen that lists what you ordered, as visual backup to what the order-taker says. Why is this so important to McDonald's? Give three reasons why you believe they recap:

1.

2.

3.

Probably the first thing that came to mind was "to ensure that the order is correct." It's a reality check. But what other reasons could there be? Here are more:

- To keep the order-taker alert
- To underscore for customers what they're getting for their money (notice that the price is only given after the recap)
- To ensure the customer's satisfaction
- To set the stage for other recommendations (e.g., fries with that Big Mac)

What McDonald's does is equally applicable to the travel sales environment. Indeed, a study at Carlson-Wagonlit Travel discovered that the simple act of recapping travel needs produces a profound and measured effect on the ability of a salesperson to get the sale.

THE SALES PROCESS AND THE BUSINESS TRAVELER

Is the sales cycle relevant to the business traveler (also known as the **corporate traveler**)? Certainly not as much as it is to someone traveling for leisure. Business travelers know where they're going and may have been there dozens of times. They often have preferred hotel chains, airlines, car rental companies—or their company has negotiated corporate rates with specific suppliers that dictate the choice.

They're less price-sensitive than leisure travelers, too, since someone else is paying (though their employer does encourage cost efficiency). The result: The travel agent who handles their account or the company person who arranges travel will operate in a service-oriented, highly transactional manner.

Yet consultative sales skills may indeed be appropriate if:

- The businessperson has never been to the destination.
- The traveler is extending the business trip for leisure purposes.
- The travel professional has some ideas or information that the corporate traveler doesn't know about that could make the trip more pleasant and productive.

Also, business travelers usually have needs that go beyond the **overt,** expected ones, like efficiency and accuracy. They may have hidden, **covert** ones, too, like the need for recognition and sympathy for all the stress that very-frequent travelers endure. Sensitive service and a bit of qualifying may enrich that businessperson's travel experience in a fundamental way.

Rule #2: Give One Recommendation; Have a Second Ready as Backup   Imagine this. You go to a travel agent and say that you're thinking of taking a tour of Europe. The agent does indeed ask you qualifying questions. He then says: "I think Trafalgar, Brendan, Insight, Tauck, and Globus Tours would all work for you. Here are brochures for each. Go through them and call me back when you decide which one you like the most and I'll be happy to book it for you."

Many flaws mark this approach to selling. What are some of the wrong effects that could come from it? Write them here:

Here are the ones we came up with:

- It requires you, the customer, to do *a lot of the research and work.*
- It *breaks the sales cycle*, allowing you to leave and return or call at a later time. Maybe you won't. Maybe you'll change your mind. Maybe you'll just book it yourself. Maybe you'll find another travel agent to do it for you.
- *You, the client, may feel perhaps more confused* than when you came in. There's such a thing as *too many* choices.
- It *erodes your confidence in the agent.*

One of the prime reasons a person contacts a travel professional is for help in making the purchase decision. The most helpful thing that the travel professional can do is to narrow the customer's choices to one or two solutions so that the decision becomes easier.

Think, now, of three things you've bought in your life where you felt you had too many choices and had a hard time selecting the right one:

1.

2.

3.

As you wrote your three examples, you probably remembered the frustration you felt back when you had to make each purchase decision. Frustration should not be what a sale is about.

A travel professional should recommend the one flight, one cruise, one tour, one hotel that fulfills the client's needs. (Of course, several hotels and places to visit are often necessary when a multi-destination trip is involved.) If the customer seems to hesitate, it may mean that she's a type who prefers to choose from several alternatives. That means your backup solution and, if necessary, a third option (if you're sure it won't confuse the client).

Moreover, you should *communicate conviction* when you recommend a travel product. It'll make your client's decision easier and help underscore your professionalism. Moreover, you must emphasize not just *what* your recommendation is about, but *why* that recommendation is the right one. Which leads us to . . .

Rule #3: Sell Benefits, Not Features   What's a **feature**? **It's a fact about the product you're selling:** the ship has five dining rooms; the car has an extra roomy trunk; this resort is right on the beach.

What's a **benefit? It's how the product affects the buyer,** why it solves his or her needs: the five dining rooms permit you to select the dining experience you want; a roomy trunk enables you to bring extra luggage; a beachside location provides a cool breeze, a great view and direct access to swimming.

Recommending through benefits is one of the most crucial things you must learn. One reason: People today don't have the imagination that people of yesteryear had. They have trouble imagining how something will benefit them.

Why? Your grandparents obtained much of their information through reading newspapers and books, talking with people, or listening to the radio. *They were forced to imagine things.*

Today, much of what we learn comes through television, CD-ROMs and the Internet. *We don't have to imagine things as much anymore.* The images are pre-formed for us, full-blown.

IT'S JUST YOUR IMAGINATION

Think of a favorite song. If you're under 40, you probably also thought of the music video that promoted it. Think of an important political event that happened recently. Odds are, the images that came to mind were ones you saw on TV. In both cases, imagination was largely unnecessary, because the media did the visualizing for you.

This poses a serious challenge to sellers of travel, since they're selling intangibles, which are inherently hard to visualize. Consumers have a difficult time translating the features that are part of your recommendation into how these features will benefit them.

SEPARATING FEATURES FROM BENEFITS

Here's a shortcut to how a benefit differs from a feature:

A feature-based statement:	**A benefit-based statement:**
• describes facts	• describes the payoff
• is impersonal	• is personal
• describes a picture	• puts the client in the picture
• rarely uses the word *you*	• frequently uses the word *you*
• is objective—it doesn't change according to the buyer	• is subjective—can vary from buyer to buyer
• tells you what it is	• tells you what it does

The well-known sales expert Zig Ziglar explains the difference between a feature and a benefit in this way: "Last year, a half-million people bought drills with 1/4" bits. But none of them wanted a drill with a 1/4" bit. They wanted a 1/4" hole."

WHAT'S A VALUE-ADDED BENEFIT?

It's **something extra you get that you ordinarily wouldn't expect:** flowers from a travel agent after you return from your cruise, free admission to an extra museum on a tour, or early admission to a theme park if you stay at one of its hotels.

The examples in the left-hand column are features from a wide spectrum of products. In the right-hand column, write what two benefits each feature might have for you:

Feature   *Benefits*

1. Your pen has a cap   A.

                                                        B.

2. Your cell phone has a bright screen   A.

                                                        B.

3. Your computer has high-speed
   Internet access

   A.

   B.

4. You'll be in Australia for 14 days

   A.

   B.

5. Your car has an alarm system

   A.

   B.

6. Your mattress is firm

   A.

   B.

7. The muffin you're eating is fat free

   A.

   B.

8. You have a lot of frequent flyer miles

A.

B.

9. Your apartment is on the top floor of a tall building

A.

B.

10. Your best friend is 6′ 8″

A.

B.

SUPER WORDS

A Yale University study found ten words to be the most persuasive. Here they are, in reverse order of effectiveness:

10. Discover(y)	5. Results
9. Love	4. New
8. Safe(ty)	3. Save
7. Health(y)	2. Money
6. Easy	1. You(r)

Note that the #1 word corroborates the other Yale study you learned about in Chapter 2.

The very same skills you just used are directly applicable to selling travel, too. (You'll have the opportunity to practice them in Activity #1 at the end of this chapter.) Always cite benefits when describing each component of your recommended trip. And as you do, remember the following:

- **Cite only the benefits that most appeal to your client.** The qualifying part of the sales cycle should give you good clues as to which benefits these are. And remember: What *you* feel may be the prime benefit *may* not *be the one your customer responds to.* Moreover, benefits of the same feature can vary from client to client. A window seat on the aircraft may appeal to one person because he likes to look out the window. Another likes it because the daylight helps her read. A third likes it because he can lean his head on the window to sleep (with a pillow for cushioning, of course). Others see a window seat as a *drawback.* They have to battle to get out of the row to visit the lavatory. So . . .
- **Preface your general benefits presentation with "Let me tell you why."** This signals to the client that you're about to explain the payoff to your recommendations.

BENEFITS OF THIS BOOK

Look back to this book's preface. It gives eight ways in which this textbook differs from others. Each bullet point gives a feature, then the benefit. See if you can distinguish between the two.

- **Be alert for drawbacks.** Drawbacks are the opposite of benefits. They're "negative benefits." When you describe a benefit and the customer counters with a valid drawback (e.g., "The hotel room is on the top floor? Sure there will be a great view, but I'll have to wait forever for the elevator! And what if there's a fire?"), you must resolve what carries more weight with the client (benefits or drawbacks), then adjust accordingly.
- **Don't oversell.** If the client seems to accept your explanation, there's no need to go on. Sure, you may feel that you need to be thorough, but if you want to tell your clients the fifteen reasons why they should go on a tour and they're convinced by the second one, stop.
- **Avoid getting lazy.** It's terribly easy to let your recommendations slacken into an inventory of features and facts. When you sense this happening to you—and it will—just remember that *benefits language can benefit you.*

Using benefit language applies to virtually all selling, not just to front-line customer interactions. If you design a Web site, create an ad, give a presentation, write a marketing plan, or talk someone into something, you'll do a better job of it—and have a better chance of getting results—if you build with benefits.

WHAT'S YOUR MOTIVE?

Benefits are closely allied to needs, or what some experts call **buying motives.** In fact, they're two sides of the same coin. *Motives are allied primarily to the buyer, benefits to the product.* For example, a person may want to buy something that makes him feel more healthy (motive). It could be a health club membership, a multiple vitamin, or a stay at a spa—each of these could *benefit* that person in a healthful way.

Here are other common motives that sellers try to fulfill, each with an example from retailing. See if you can come up with a travel product that also fulfills these needs:

Motive/need:	Product/service that fulfills it:	Travel product that fulfills it:
1. Safety/security/peace of mind	Guaranteed savings account	
2. Convenience	A cell phone	
3. Flexibility	A Swiss Army knife	
4. Pleasure/fun	A video game	
5. Money savings	A clothing sale	
6. Time savings	The Yellow Pages	
7. Status	A Rolex watch	
8. Recognition	An employee of the month award	

Rule #4: Paint Customers into the Picture Intimately allied to selling via benefits, this tactic focuses on getting clients to picture themselves on the trip you're suggesting. If they've never taken a cruise before (90 percent of the public hasn't), it will be difficult for them to take the leap mentally from your recommendation to reality. They have no experience to draw from. They can't picture it. Moreover, it's an intangible, an experience, something inherently hard to visualize.

How can you help? The word *you* is a great start. So, too, is *when*, rather than *if*. For example, "When you take this cruise" will more easily lead to a buy than "If you take this cruise."

Words that are visual add zest to your recommendation: "The rooms in this Westin are really beautiful and spacious. And wait till you see the view." It's almost impossible *not* to see that room. In fact, you feel like *you own it already*.

WORDS THAT MAKE YOU MOVE

People don't go somewhere just to see something, but also to *do* something. If you describe to your client how he's engaging in an activity within the picture you've painted, you'll bring it to life. Remember: Real life moves.

Rule #5: Hit Their Hot Buttons   Remember what you learned about hot buttons in Chapter 2? In any qualifying session, you'll find hot buttons tucked beneath the more obvious needs that the client has. A hot button is a sort of "super benefit" that strongly seizes a customer's attention. In fact, it's the one you should lead with when making your recommendation, since it will most directly lead to the sale.

Just as drawbacks are the opposite of benefits, **cold buttons** are the opposite of hot buttons. They're things that strongly turn off the customer and can defeat the sale. If you encounter a cold button ("I hate mass-market destinations"), strive to fashion a travel experience that avoids what the client dislikes and plays to what she prefers.

Rule #6: Exile Jargon from Your Vocabulary   Try a little exercise. In the space below, write a sentence that uses so much jargon that a person not familiar with the industry it comes from could make no sense of it. It can be something from a previous job of yours or from a specialized interest (e.g., from skiing, the term *ski in/ski out*).

What you've just written is the equivalent of the following from air travel:

"The K and V seats are sold out, so you have to take an H seat with a 50 percent penalty instead of an NR."

It's incredibly easy to fall into opaque language like this. It's like putting up a screen between you and your client, a barrier that the client is afraid to ask about or mention. Just remember: People don't buy from people they don't understand.

Rule #7: Tailor to Type   Did you ever buy a "one-size-fits-all" bathrobe, only to discover you looked like Mickey Mouse in his Sorcerer's Apprentice outfit?

In selling, no one approach fits all. Qualifying should give you clear clues that enable you to adjust to your client's style.

THE WILLINGHAM TYPES

Author Ron Willingham divides buyers into four categories. Here are each type's characteristics, with allied travel recommendations:

Type	Traits	Travel recommendations
The Talker (Think Willard Scott)	• Sociable • Family-oriented • Talkative	• Tours • Cruises • Family travel • Leisure add-on to business trip
The Doer (Think Donald Trump)	• Ambitious • Time-pressed • Proud of achievements • Makes gut decisions	• Higher class of product • Meet-and-greet services • Flexible arrangements
The Controller (Think Felix Unger of *The Odd Couple*)	• Logical/methodical • Organized • Efficient • Not impulsive	• Stress cost savings • Organized travel (e.g., cruises, tours) • Well-researched itineraries
The Diligent (Think Homer Simpson)	• Likes predictability • Indecisive • Creature of habit • Trusting • Safety-conscious	• Well-known product brands • Large rental cars • All-suite hotels • Travel insurance

---

Rule #8: Sell to Their Needs, Not Yours   Have you ever said, "If only everybody thought like me?" They don't. And so it bears repeating: You must recommend what your customers will like, not what you like. Keep in mind:

- We tend to recommend places we know well and love.
- We tend to interpret travel experiences according to the activities we ourselves prefer and the values we hold.
- We favor suppliers we're comfortable with and especially those with personnel we may know and like.

Shifting perspective from your own to that of another—to "ego shift"—is one of the most challenging things that a salesperson can do. Yet it's central to caring salesmanship.

PLAYING FAVORITES

Answer the following questions:

1. Which brand of soft drink do you usually prefer?

2. Which make of car do you think is the best?

3. What's your favorite movie of all time?

Again, in selling it usually doesn't matter what you want, it's what the *buyer* wants. Two sales situations, however, do in fact require you to play favorites.

In the first type, a travel seller offers only one brand in each category of product. This is called an **exclusive supplier relationship.** For instance, at Walt Disney World you can only buy Coca Cola, but at a Marriott hotel you can only get Pepsi. Other examples:

- AAA provides only American Express traveler's checks to its members.
- Carlson-Wagonlit Travel sells only Access America travel insurance.
- Crystal Cruises provides only Caesars Palace gaming onboard its ships.
- Certain airports allow only one product brand to have locations within its facilities: Several Starbucks but no Coffee Bean, two McDonald's but no Burger King, Wetzel's Pretzels but no Auntie Anne's.

Such exclusive relationships usually involve very simple commodities (travel-related or otherwise) and require almost no sales skills on the part of the intermediary, except, perhaps, the ability to deflect a customer's concern about having only one choice.

An exclusive supplier relationship offers three major advantages to the intermediary company:

- The price the intermediary pays for the supplier's products and services is deeply discounted or the commission derived is very high. It's what the supplier agrees to for the benefit of exclusivity.
- The supplier is more likely to provide cooperative (co-op) promotional monies to the intermediary to support their joint efforts. (In most cases the intermediary must, in return, prominently mention that it provides the supplier's product.)

- Communication between the supplier and the intermediary is smooth and problem resolution is usually easy.

The second type of supplier-intermediary relationship is the **preferred** one. In this model, the intermediary offers most travel products for sale, but recommends certain ones over others. Here's a nontravel example: Circuit City emphasizes Panasonic large-screen TV products, though it also sells Sony.

Can you think of another example? You may have to browse through a newspaper to come up with one. Once you do, write it here:

The same thing happens in the travel industry. For example, a tour operator that offers independent tours to Hawaii may highlight Sheraton Hotels in its brochures, though the company also lists and offers Hilton and Aston properties. To address its guests' upscale needs, Seabourn Cruise Lines offers many Ritz-Carlton properties as part of its pre- and postcruise packages. Thrifty Car Rental features quality products of Daimler Chysler and other fine cars. (This last example is a little different, though, since the customer may not have much choice as to which brand he rents.)

Car rentals are a significant part of the travel business. *(Courtesy of Thrifty Car Rental)*

The preferred supplier model especially predominates in the travel agency marketplace. Though most travel agencies sell all brands of travel products (or at least the ones they feel are reliable), they usually limit their initial recommendation to certain favored suppliers. Preferred suppliers usually contract with the chain or **consortium** that the agency belongs to, with the understanding that the supplier will provide certain favored benefits to that agency in return for preferred status. Among these possible benefits:

- Higher commissions
- Special client benefits (e.g., an automatic upgrade to a higher level, like a one-class car rental or one-category stateroom upgrade, at no extra cost)
- Co-op advertising funds
- A brand name that's perhaps well known to the public
- Easier access to sales reps
- Easier problem resolution
- An exclusive telephone number to make reservations
- Invitations to special training programs
- Better access to industry-only discounted travel
- Greater ease in mastering the products sold (a travel agent can't be an expert on the hundreds of products out there, but she can be an expert on those limited preferred products that the agency sells)

Here's the ideal lineup of preferred suppliers a travel agency typically has:

- One car rental company
- One or two airlines (though airlines rarely set up preferred agreements with agencies)
- Two or three hotel chains (each perhaps representing a different value level)
- One travel insurance company
- Two or three major cruise lines at different value levels (or one family of cruise lines, where several brands are owned by one company)
- One independent tour operator
- Two escorted tour operators
- Three or four special-interest tour operators, cruise lines and other suppliers (e.g., those that are adventure, family, ecotourism or youth-oriented)

But isn't steering customers to preferred suppliers manipulative and counterproductive to serving a client's needs? And if a supplier uses incentives to get a tour operator or travel agency to favor its products over others, does that benefit the traveling public?

Consider the following: The typical physician prescribes only eighteen drugs. Doctors find that they can successfully treat most ills with a limited number of medications, drawn from favored pharmaceutical companies. But when a patient needs something that's outside those eighteen, the physician will indeed go beyond the eighteen and find the drug that's appropriate.

So, too, will travel consultants. Agencies, tour operators and, in some cases, cruise lines strive to assemble a limited collection of trusted, high-quality preferreds that solve the needs of, say, 80 percent of their customers. They'll turn to suppliers outside that selection only when:

- Their preferred suppliers have nothing available on the dates the customer has requested.
- The rate which the preferred supplier has quoted is substantially higher than what a non-preferred is offering for a similar category (e.g., Hertz's rate for a certain time, city, and car category is $289, while Dollar is offering the same for $198).
- The experience the client requires is not satisfied in any way by a preferred (e.g., she wants a downtown hotel but the preferreds only have properties in suburban areas).
- The preferred supplier's option in a certain situation is highly inferior to that of a non-preferred (e.g., the preferred's air itinerary requires two connections, while the non-preferred's is nonstop).
- The client strongly feels that a certain nonpreferred product is the one he wants, even when the travel agent has carefully pointed out the benefits that the preferred offers.

In almost all other situations, offering solutions exclusively from among preferred suppliers makes total sense.

Converting Buyers

Have you ever had your mind set on buying a certain brand of product, only to have the salesperson convince you to buy another? Try to remember one instance where this happened and describe it below, along with what the salesperson did to make you change your mind:

What you've just described is called **converting the buyer.** (It's not to be confused with *sales conversion,* a marketing term that usually applies to the percentage of customers who show interest versus those who actually buy.) Converting the buyer can occur:

1. When the buyer has one brand in mind and the seller converts him to a preferred one.
2. When the buyer has one type of travel in mind (e.g., air and car rental) and the seller converts that buyer to a package, such as a tour or a cruise.

3. When the buyer wants a clearly inferior brand and the seller offers a much better one.

Converting is a very delicate process. The key: Don't make buyers feel badly about their original idea. Here's the way to do it:

1. Affirm that their original choice is a good one (unless, of course, it clearly isn't).
2. Ask why they chose it. Be alert to dubious reasons (e.g., the ad looked good; a friend recommended it—but does the friend have similar interests?).
3. Explain that you have an alternate suggestion, point out the benefits similar to the one the clients cited for their original choice, then underscore whatever *added benefits* your recommendation offers.
4. Say that you think your recommendation might better serve their needs.
5. Ask them what they'd now like to do.

More often than not, your conversion will work. If it doesn't, you still have a good probability of a sale.

The trickiest conversion of all is when the customer is strongly loyal to a product that's different from the one that you, the seller, have in mind. You must affirm the clients' opinions and explore why they're loyal to that brand (but without indicating initially that you may suggest something else). Agree with their choice (unless it's *really* wrong). Don't contradict them. Then ask if they're open to a change of pace. If they are, then go into your usual recommendation process. If they're not open to change, then simply sell them what they want.

SALES PRESENTATIONS

A sales presentation can mean many things. It can be a synonym for the sales process in general or apply specifically to the recommendation phase. In travel, however, as in many businesses, it usually refers to *a presentation made in the business-to-business or within-business sales models*. Some examples of sales presentations:

- An Amtrak executive explains to a group of senior management officials why a high-speed train between Los Angeles and Las Vegas makes great financial sense.
- A cruise line sales representative explains to a gathering of travel agents how several new itineraries will benefit them and their clients.
- A salesperson at a convention center sends a written proposal to a professional organization, spelling out why its facility represents the best venue for their next conference. (This is usually in response to an **RFP,** or **Request for Proposal.**)

Sales presentations of this kind often follow a set of strategies that parallels the regular sales cycle. They also—as you can tell from the above examples—take two forms: oral and written. We'll address presentation *writing* style in Chapter 7. But let's look at some tactics that work for *oral* presentations.

Oral Sales Presentations

Here are six strategies that mark the best oral presentations, no matter how large the size of the audience:

1. **Keep it brief.** People's attention spans today are short. Keep each section tight and get to the point.
2. **Back it up with visuals.** One study discovered that 86 percent of the information we absorb is visual. PowerPoint or similar graphic presentation programs have become a near-essential part of today's presentations. (Flipcharts, whiteboard, slides, and transparencies are acceptable alternatives in certain situations.)
3. **Create interaction.** Just as in a front-line-to-the-public sale, presentations are always more powerful if the audience is actually involved in what's going on, with the presenter asking questions and eliciting responses.
4. **Address different thinking styles.** Within your audience may be all sorts of cognitive styles. So balance your facts and figures with anecdotal examples and, if appropriate, humor.
5. **Mix it up.** An oral sales presentation should not be entirely predictable. Shift from on-screen graphics to a flipchart. Ask questions, present, go back to questions. People absorb information more easily and are more attentive if they don't exactly know what's coming next.
6. **Link benefits to features.** Yes, it's the same strategy that salespeople use with individuals. Presenters must clarify *why* the recommendations are the right ones.

ADDRESSING CONCERNS

Imagine that someone has suggested you should take an escorted motor-coach tour. What concerns might you have about that suggestion? List two here:

1.

2.

It's rare that a recommendation doesn't provoke at least a few buyer concerns. A salesperson must be prepared to counter whatever objection a customer may bring up. And someone shaping a company's marketing must adjust for these potential roadblocks, too.

Now's the time to try your hand at it. Take the two concerns you listed above and come up with what a salesperson might say to overcome each objection:

1.

2.

A seller's counter to an objection—the fourth step in our sales cycle—should take into consideration which of the following categories the concern falls into:

1. **A real objection is one based on fact.** The concern that, say, an escorted tour limits the flexibility of a person's trip is usually true. One response: Point out that you can suggest a tour that's much more flexible than most, with plenty of free time and options. If that fails, go to another recommendation.
2. **A hidden objection** is one based on reality, but which the buyer doesn't want to reveal or admit to. For example, the client may be somewhat shy—the socializing that occurs on a tour is highly stressful to that person. Customers with hidden concerns will give some other reason to camouflage the real one. If your counter doesn't work, this may be the reason. Go on to another recommendation.
3. **An imaginary objection** is one based on misinformation or a falsehood. The client might say, "But tours are expensive." The response: "Most tours—when you consider what they include and offer—are an excellent value." (And you go on to prove it.)

Travel professionals who have been in the business for a while have heard a standard set of objections over and over. These experiences help them become adept at solving familiar concerns and eventually settling on the counters they've found work the best.

The Process of Solving Concerns

Overcoming objections should follow a certain sequence, similar to what you learned to convert buyers. It's sometimes called the PASS formula. Here it is, with an example on how to defuse a customer's concern that "cruises are boring."

Paraphrase:	"Oh, you're concerned that there won't be enough for you to do."
Agree with the feeling:	"I understand. You did say you wanted an active vacation."
Show the truth:	"That's exactly why I'm recommending a cruise to you." (Then show an activity log from an actual cruise.) Note: Don't use the word *but*. It implies that the customer's feelings are wrong.
Seek feedback:	"So, what do you think?"

Another, similar technique to solve concerns is called the 3F solution. It uses three words beginning with the letter *f*: feel, felt, found. An example:

- I see why you **feel** that there's not much to do in Canada.
- I **felt** that way, too.
- Then I went and **found** out that there were countless things to do and see in Canada.

If, however, your efforts fail to solve the concern, don't keep at it. There are times when you must quietly and simply shift to another recommendation that defuses the client's objections. Only in that way will you be able to finally connect with your customers.

Name: _____ Date: _____

ACTIVITY #1   SELL THOSE BENEFITS

In the left-hand columns is a list of travel-related features. Try to spell out a benefit for each.

Feature   **Benefit**

1. The seats in business class recline 45 degrees.

2. This cruise ship goes fast.

3. At this resort, all meals are included.

4. The train goes from mid-town New York City to Boston's city center.

5. The tour manager takes care of everything.

6. The phone in your hotel room has a 25-foot cord.

7. The restaurant is buffet-style.

8. A tour guide will take us through the Colosseum.

9. The rollercoaster's first hill is 300 feet high.

10. You have the option of purchasing car rental insurance.

Name: _____   Date: _____

ACTIVITY #2   JETTISON JARGON

Travel industry terminology can certainly confuse a customer. It even occasionally confuses travel professionals. Based on what you already know about the industry or from informed sources (an introductory travel book, knowledgeable friends, etc.), explain in layman's terms each of the following:

Phrase   **Explanation**

  1. A PNR

  2. A concierge-level room

  3. An open-jaw itinerary

  4. An all-inclusive resort

  5. A double-double room

  6. A suite

  7. A 767

  8. Space is available

  9. Second seating

 10. CDW

Name: _____   Date: _____

ACTIVITY #3   CRUISE SOLUTIONS

Based on your knowledge of cruising (or, if necessary, research), try to create a solution to each of the following objections to cruising:

Objection   **Solution**

1. Cruises are too expensive.

2. Only old people cruise.

3. Cruises are too organized and regimented.

4. I'll get seasick.

5. There isn't much for kids to do.

6. You don't have time to really experience a port.

7. I'll eat too much.

8. The cabins are too small and confining.

4

Enhancing the Sale and Achieving an Agreement

OBJECTIVES

After reading this chapter, you'll be able to:

- Cross-sell travel products

- Apply seven strategies to successful upselling

- Achieve an agreement and close the sale

- Practice four "little steps" of selling

Why would you go to a Burger King? Or your local cineplex? Or to a car wash? Your probable answers: to buy a hamburger, to see a movie, and to have your car cleaned, of course.

Yes, people go to Burger King to buy hamburgers. And in Burger King's early years, hamburgers were *the* profit center. But competition forced down the cost of hamburgers. It's not unusual today for Burger King to occasionally offer its hamburgers for 69¢. You don't make money on a 69¢ sandwich.

So the hamburger—especially when it's sold at a promotional price—becomes a loss leader. (**A loss leader is something that produces little, no or negative profit, but draws people in, where they're likely to buy**

other, more profitable things.) Burger King, however, trains its salespeople to suggest additional items, like fries, shakes, and desserts. If the customer fails to order a beverage, the employee will remind him. The salesperson also might suggest some sort of "value meal" package that includes the hamburger, fries, and a drink (getting you to buy more than you may have intended to). Or she might ask if the customer would rather have their famous bigger hamburger, the Whopper.

A parallel situation occurs at movie theaters. Here's a little known fact: Your local cineplex most likely makes *all* of its profits at the concession stand, where you happily buy a candy bar, hot dog, soda, or tub of popcorn for as much as *ten times* what you'd normally pay. The price of admission only serves to offset the theater's salaries, overhead, and the right to exhibit the movie.

And what about car washes? Same thing. If you didn't buy the gas, the wax option, car fresheners, and greeting cards that the car wash makes available for purchase, the car wash would probably go out of business.

Clearly, selling extras and higher levels of products is essential to profitability in almost any field—including travel. But is it ethical? Yes, *so long as it enhances the client's satisfaction*. A beverage does indeed "help the food go down." Wax does protect a car's finish. And fresh popcorn does seem to make for a happier movie experience. That's why we call this fifth step in the sales cycle *enhancing the sale*. Enhancing the sale is divided into cross-selling, upselling, and package-selling.

CROSS-SELLING

Before understanding what a cross-sell is, it's important to define a core-sell. **A core-sell is selling what a customer came to you to buy.** In our three opening examples, the customers wanted to purchase a hamburger, a movie admission, and a car wash. These were the core products. They're the obvious ones.

However, these customers also bought fries, popcorn, and an air freshener. These are called cross-sells. **A cross-sell occurs when a seller offers a buyer the opportunity to purchase allied products that go beyond the obvious core products.** They're the "side dishes," the extras. See if you can find examples of cross-sells in the following core-purchase situations:

Situation	*Cross-sell example*
1. You're buying a car	
2. You're buying a dress or suit	

3. You're ordering new
   eyeglasses

4. You're having your teeth
   cleaned

5. You're on an airplane

6. You're buying flowers at a
   florist

7. You're getting a CD player

8. You've signed up for golf
   lessons

9. You're buying a pair of shoes

10. You've enlisted in a weight-
    loss program

Is each of the examples you gave above an "extra"? If it is, it's a cross-sell. Do you see the value in buying each? If so, then each example would genuinely enhance the purchase. Be careful, though. If any of your examples raises the quality or cost of the core product (e.g., you buy a better car), that's not a cross-sell. It's probably an upsell, which you'll learn more about later in this chapter.

ACTIVE AND PASSIVE CROSS-SELLING

Cross-selling is **active when the customer buys the additional product because the seller has suggested it.** For instance, a reservationist might suggest travel insurance, something the client would probably not have thought of.

Cross-selling is **passive when the idea of purchasing something extra occurs to the buyer without a salesperson initiating it.** Examples of passive cross-sells:

- You ask an auto rental serviceperson about the availability of an in-car mapping/positioning system and what the daily rate for it would be.
- You buy a TV Guide at the supermarket checkout stand only because you happen to see it.
- You buy flight insurance because at the airport you pass a machine that issues flight insurance.
- You upgrade to a concierge-level hotel room because a sign at the check-in counter says "Ask about our special rates on our upgraded rooms."

The last three examples are **impulse buys.** (An impulse buy implies little customer planning, careful placement and, usually, low cost.)

Cross-Selling and Travel

Razor-thin profit margins on core products (especially airline tickets) have made cross-selling a required survival skill in the travel industry. Cross-selling is now integral to virtually every segment of the travel industry. Travel lends itself so easily to cross-selling because it's rare that a person buys one travel component without buying another. Economists would therefore say that travel is a **complementary business, where one purchase automatically leads to other, related ones.**

Even if you buy only a flight and intend to stay with relatives, you're still going to have to get to and from the airport somehow, buy some meals, and perhaps pay admission fees to attractions—all potential cross-sell items.

Let's do an exercise that's somewhat similar to the previous one, but uses only travel-related examples. Fill out the right-hand column with one example for each situation:

Situation	*Cross-sell example*
1. The customer is at the National airport counter and rents a car. You, the sales representative offer . . .	

2. Two novice skiers drive to a local mountain resort and purchase lift tickets. You, who sold the lift tickets to them, suggest . . .

3. A passenger is on an escorted motorcoach tour. You, the tour escort, offer . . .

4. A client buys a Princess cruise from a travel agency. You, the travel agent, offer . . .

5. You, the hotel's poolside attendant, provide towels for a couple. You suggest . . .

You may have noticed several things when completing the above. First, a cross-sell may occur even when a free core service is rendered. The towels at the pool are free; it's the job of the pool attendant to hand them out. However, pool attendants often cross-sell such items as tanning lotion, sunglasses and, in some cases, sports equipment rentals.

A similar situation exists with a hotel concierge. In theory, the concierge gives advice and assistance free of charge (though tipping is often expected). When a concierge suggests and offers to book something that the client will pay for (e.g., theater tickets, a hotel-airport transfer, or a city tour), he is indeed acting as a salesperson and is cross-selling.

PROMPTING

Cross-sales have become so important to profitability that GDS screens remind reservationists and travel agents to offer them. For example, after booking a flight, airline reservationists are sometimes reminded by their computers to ask the traveler if he needs a car rental. Such on-screen cues are sometimes called **prompts.**

This brings up another question that the previous exercise may have triggered. Who makes the extra money that a cross-sell generates? That depends. In some cases (e.g., when a flight attendant sells movie headsets), the company that employs the salesperson makes all the profit. In other, rarer cases, it's the salesperson who makes the profit. For instance, concierges usually receive the full commission from any paid service they arrange for the hotel's guests. They don't have to share it with the hotel. (Often these commissions, as well as tips, are pooled for distribution among all concierges. Front desk staff may even receive a portion of these concierge profits, too.)

In many situations, however, both employer and employee make money. The seller receives his or her portion in the form of a bonus, incentive fee, or percentage of commission; the rest of the profit goes to the company.

For instance, workers at a car rental desk may get a cash bonus for each "full gas tank" option they sell. Some travel agents receive a bonus (e.g., $10) or as much as half the commission on each travel insurance policy they sell. Tour managers get a commission for each optional tour they book (e.g., a nightclub tour not on the itinerary). Such arrangements give an incentive to front-liners to cross-sell at each and every customer interaction.

MORE THAN EXTRAS

Many travel agents would say that airline tickets are their core product (despite the low profit involved). Clients who contact travel agencies, though, may have "extras" more in mind than travel agents think. Here's what customers wanted advice on from their travel agents, according to a 2000 *Travel Weekly* magazine poll:

1. Hotels (68%)
2. Package tours (66%)
3. Car rentals (56%)
4. Destinations (56%)
5. Airline tickets (54%)

Cross-Sell Reluctance

Many travel professionals feel awkward about cross-selling, despite the fact that it may enhance their paychecks. What are the reasons?

1. **Some salespeople are under the misapprehension that cross-sells are merely a profit center for their companies and/or for themselves.** Out of customer concern, they don't want their clients to pay more money than they have to. Yet that cross-sell may very well be a benefit in the eyes of the client. Also, buyers of travel don't always know what a salesperson is able to offer. They don't realize that an airline reservationist can book a car rental for them or that a travel agent can, say, sell them admissions to Universal Studios.
2. **The salesperson believes that cross-selling is manipulative and unethical.** If the cross-sell tricks a customer into buying more things than he wanted to or *is able to*, then that cross-sale is ethically dubious. If its intent is convenience, vacation improvement, or building value into the purchase, then it's a positive thing to do.
3. **Salespeople sometimes have incomplete knowledge of and/or experience with the cross-sell items.** A cross-sell suggestion can unleash a slew of questions. Is the seller ready for them? Here, product training is a must.
4. **The salesperson hasn't fully explored the customer's needs.** A cross-sell that's not anchored to a full understanding of a buyer's motives

and plans can seem "tacked on." Conversely, if you don't know much about the customer, it's hard to know which cross-sells to offer.

HOW TRAVEL BUSINESSES MAKE MONEY

Most travel suppliers operate as any other business would: They figure out all their costs, then sell at a price that yields a preset profit margin. (The profit margin, of course, may vary according to the product, time of the year, etc.)

Travel agencies operate differently. Rather than purchasing airline tickets, hotel stays, car rentals, cruises and tours at a net (noncommissionable) rate, then marking them up for resale to the public, travel agencies usually sell at a price established by the supplier, then receive a commission back at a later time. (In some cases the supplier allows agencies to deduct the commission before sending in payment.) Typical commission rates that travel agencies receive:

- Hotels: 10%
- Car rentals: 10%
- Tours: 10–16%
- Cruises: 10–16%
- Travel insurance: 20–35%
- Air: 5–10%, usually with "caps" on the maximum commission (for airlines that still pay commission; most major U.S. airlines have eliminated commissions)

Some industry experts believe that net pricing, with markups, will eventually replace the current, commission-based travel agency model.

One major recommendation, unless there's no choice: *Cross-selling should be fully integrated into the sales process*. It should not feel like an "Oh, here's something else I'd like to sell to you" sort of thing. For example, a good clothing salesperson won't sell a suit to a buyer and then, just before ringing up the sale on the register, suggest a tie or shirt to go with it. A salesperson who knows what he's doing will bring out a few ties and shirts (but not too many) during the selection process to help the buyer judge the color-matching attributes of the suit. The buyer later will be more likely to purchase that tie and shirt than if they were offered only at the end.

The same applies to travel. Cross-selling opportunities occur *throughout the sales cycle*, not just toward the end. Say a client calls an independent tour operator with diversified offerings. She mentions that she wishes she could see France in some novel way. This moment might be the time (depending on the client's interests, budget and personality) for a reservationist to bring up a barge cruise, high-speed rail option, or a Bombard Society hot-air balloon trip.

Note, too, that *you can cross-sell a destination*. If you were a travel agent, you could suggest to Australia-bound clients that they stop over in New Zealand and/or Fiji along the way. It enhances the clients' trip (they may not go that far, in that direction, again for many years to come). It probably will enhance the agency's profits, too, since the added destinations may extend the trip and require more hotel nights.

CROSS-SELLING INSURANCE

One of the most beneficial and profitable cross-sells in the travel industry is travel insurance. Two types exist: the kind offered by a supplier (e.g., a cruise line, tour company or car rental firm) or a policy from a third-party insurance company. Supplier reservationists or desk service-people (e.g., at car rental firms) are usually taught to offer their company's insurance to buyers, since the profit margin is excellent. Travel agents, too, sometimes sell supplier insurance (it's simpler to book the supplier's product and its insurance in one transaction). But most travel agents favor third-party insurance, since the commissions are usually higher and, if the supplier goes bankrupt, the insurance covers any monetary loss. (Supplier insurance usually becomes worthless if that supplier defaults.)

Travel insurance offers three major advantages to travelers:

- It protects the customer from on-trip hassles and unanticipated costs.
- It helps reduce client travel anxiety.
- It frequently provides a 24/7 assistance center that can help the traveler if problems occur.

It also benefits the seller:

- The profit from the sale is very high.
- It positions the seller as a full-service provider.
- It deflects the problem-solving from the seller to the insurance fulfillment service.
- It paints the seller and/or supplier as the solution, rather than the source, of any problem that may arise.

UPSELLING

Upselling (or selling up) is offering a buyer the opportunity to purchase a higher, more expensive level of product than the buyer had in mind. As with cross-sells, upselling sometimes makes sales professionals uncomfortable. They may have limited knowledge and experience with what they're recommending, have not really explored what quality level the customer is accustomed to, do it only toward the end of the sale or feel that it's manipulative.

Try this exercise. On the left, list as many things you can think of that you've purchased and wish you had bought at a higher quality level than you did (e.g., a faster computer). On the right, list all the things you've purchased that you regret having bought at a higher quality level (e.g., a $100 pen that feels and writes only a little better than a $3.69 one).

I wish I had bought these at a higher quality level:

I wish I had bought these at a lower quality level:

Almost surely your list on the right was harder to compile than the one on the left. The reason: People usually are pleased and more satisfied by the most expensive level of product they can afford. The finest, highest priced model of Whirlpool dishwasher receives the best satisfaction rate of any of its models. The most comprehensive home insurance plan possible provokes the fewest complaints. And ask any tour manager: The more expensive a tour, the easier it is to please the passengers. Of course, high-cost but low-quality products unleash the most passionate complaints of all. If you pay a lot, you expect quality and excellence, and rightly so.

Upselling isn't always appropriate, though. Certain customers—the extremely price-sensitive—put such a premium on low prices that selling them lower-level products, rather than the best, is probably the right thing to do. (Hint: It's extremely difficult to make money from the price-sensitive, unless you do *huge* volume and operate at peak efficiency. Moreover, price-sensitive customers are loyal to price, rather than to the company they buy from. Repeat business occurs only if the supplier consistently provides the lowest prices.)

Secrets of Successful Upselling

At a car rental location, a service agent suggests a convertible instead of an intermediate-size car. On the phone, a hotel reservationist recommends to a family of three a suite rather than a standard-size room. In a negotiation session, a resort sales manager convinces a tour planner that for a few dollars more, tour participants can have rooms with a spectacular view. In a cruise counseling session, a travel agent lists the advantages of an outside stateroom with verandah to a honeymoon couple. A hotel concierge recommends a private tour in a car with a driver and

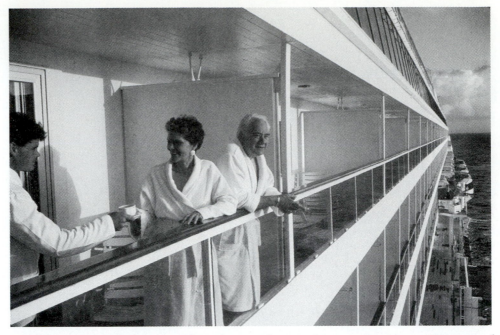

Crystal Cruises provides a significantly upscale experience to its guests. *(Courtesy of Crystal Cruises)*

guide, instead of a city motorcoach tour. And at a theme park, a ticket-seller suggests a VIP ticket that will enable the visitors to bypass waiting lines.

All these are prime examples of upselling. But to profit from upselling, it's critical that you know exactly how to do it. Here are seven tips:

1. **Understand your customer's price expectations.** As you learned in Chapter 2, you must—especially in consultative selling—obtain a realistic idea of what the buyer's budget range is. Never ask: "How much do you want to spend?" The client's answer will probably be below what he is really prepared to spend. A "budget range" query will give you a truer snapshot of the customer's financial resources for this trip.

2. **Aim high.** The top figure your client gives may, intentionally, be a bit low. Take that into consideration. But don't try to upsell to a level unreasonably higher than what was set as an upper limit. Your job is to serve your buyers, not bankrupt them.

3. **Stress value.** As you go up the quality ladder, benefits sometimes increase even more quickly. Remind the customer of all that she'll get from this better purchase.

4. **Sell out of their wallet, not yours.** Travel professionals often assume that the public will spend about the same as *they* would on travel. They forget two things: that travel salespersons like themselves often travel at a greatly reduced rate and that certain customers may make more money than they do. To a travel professional, an Inter-Continental hotel room is worth, say, an industry rate of $189 nightly, but to a regular, upscale businessperson, that same Inter-Continental room might feel like a bargain at $319. Repeated experiences with price-sensitive shoppers may skew the salesperson's thinking, too. Not everyone

HOW THE WEALTHY THINK

There's an old saying: "The rich don't think like you or me." Here are some of the needs of upscale travel customers:

- **Quality** and **excellence** are more important than price to them. They want the best.
- They're **loyal** customers to those who do their job well.
- They expect **high levels of attention** and service.
- They seek **value.** For example, they like the idea of getting a $600-per-night room for, say, $450.
- They **complain less** (unless, of course, their experience is terribly botched—they do have high expectations).
- They're **active** travelers. They want to *do* as well as to see.
- They collect **unique experiences.** Mass-market destinations generally don't appeal to them. Nepal, Botswana, and Uruguay might.
- They want to **learn.** A relentless quest for knowledge probably propelled them to success. That same passion applies to their travels.
- They prefer **exclusivity.** The idea of a product that's not available to most people appeals to them. Admission to a private garden, limo service, a private jet trip, insider tips on a destination—these are the types of experiences and services they seek.
- They enjoy **meeting their peers.** This is why they're quite willing to share a super-luxury cruise with hundreds of people, since those hundreds are as wealthy as they are. Indeed, they're fascinated by how these people achieved their success.

wants a $110-per-person per-day cruise rate. Some want a *$600-per-person per-day cruise rate.*

5. **Be alert for special occasions.** People who are celebrating a special occasion, like a honeymoon, anniversary or birthday, often want to be upsold. They typically spend far more on a special-occasion trip than they would on a "regular" vacation. Romantic couples, people who are pursuing a special interest or hobby and, interestingly, people who have recently conquered a life-threatening illness or event are especially willing to spend extra on a vacation.

6. **Tell them they deserve a special trip.** Some people are reluctant to spend extra discretionary dollars to make their vacation better. They feel guilty about buying personal luxuries, *even if they have the money to do so.* Such clients are usually resistant to upselling, but *you never know.* Sometimes all they need to hear is "You only live once" or "You worked hard for this. You deserve it."

7. **Move them from the left brain to the right.** You've probably heard about the research done in the 1970s which indicated that each side of the brain is specialized: the left side is rational, linear, and math-oriented, while the right side is more emotional, artistic, holistic, and intuitive. This cognitive model turned out to be simplistic, but, in general, it works.

When customers buy travel, they're usually in a left-brain, "I don't want to pay anything more than this" frame of mind. Yet the left brain doesn't go on vacation. It's the *right brain*, the part that's saying, "Ooh, I wish I could stay in an ocean-view suite at that super-deluxe resort

Honeymoon couples want their post-wedding travel vacation to be extra special. *(Courtesy of Keii and Patricia Johnston)*

on St. Martin, then I'll drive around in my rent-a-Mercedes convertible." The trick: to get customers to shift, at least a little, into their right-brain thinking. Some of the recommending strategies you learned in Chapter 3—use benefits, paint pictures, use power words, and hit their hot buttons—will help that process along.

And don't worry. If you suggest too pricey a package, the left brain will restore a dose of reality to both buyer and seller.

Upselling can genuinely enhance a traveler's trip. If you've qualified the client well, upselling opportunities should come easily and naturally.

PACKAGE-SELLING

You've heard the saying "big things come in small packages." In travel, big profits come in not-so-small packages. **A travel package is one in which the supplier has bundled several travel components into one product.** The two most obvious examples of packaged travel are tours and cruises, which provide lodging, transportation, meals, entertainment, and other elements for one price. Just about any travel segment, however, offers some form of travel packages. Airlines, rail operators, hotels (especially all-inclusives), ski resorts, and many others have discovered the powerful appeal of packages.

Why do consumers like packages? Because packages:

- Enable buyers to know up-front what their costs will be (the United States Tour Operators Association has calculated that the typical package saves the consumer about 15 to 20 percent compared to an FIT-type trip)

- Usually represent superb values (e.g., an independent tour to Hawaii or Mexico that includes air, lodging, and transfers may be less expensive than the air purchased alone)
- Reduce logistic hassles once the travelers get to their destination

---

MINI ACTIVITY: LET'S GO TO HAWAII

Try to obtain a brochure of a large wholesaler to Hawaii, such as Pleasant Hawaiian Holidays, Classic Custom Vacations, or SunTrips. Find the lowest price for a week-long fly-drive package to Hawaii. (You may find this in the Sunday newspaper, too.) What is the price, what departure/return dates does it apply to and what does it include? Now call an airline and find out what the round-trip airfare to/from Hawaii would be for that same time period. What do you conclude? Write your answer here:

Why do *travel professionals* also like to sell packages?

- They're easy to sell. (According to the National Tour Association, the typical FIT takes twelve hours to arrange.)
- They usually produce more profit. By selling packages, for example, travel agents get commission on almost everything the client does, often at a commission rate of 12 to 15 percent. And the supplier (e.g., the tour operator or cruise line) has so much more to make money from.
- They often tap hard-to-access inventory. Package operators often tie up air, hotel, and other travel components for up to thirty days before departure. (Now you know why additional seats on certain flights suddenly become available about a month before the flight takes place.)

As airlines have reduced or eliminated commissions to travel agencies, agents have begun to shift their selling from a la carte, FIT solutions to packages. (If you obtain your air from the tour company or other packager, you typically get 10 percent commission on that air. That's much better than what the airlines offer.) This agent commitment to selling packages has, in turn, led to healthy growth rates for almost all packagers of travel.

ACHIEVING AN AGREEMENT

All that you've learned up to now about selling is useless unless it leads to one thing: the sale itself. Unless your customer buys, what you've done is provide that client with service, understanding, perhaps even inspiration—and all for free (or even worse, the customer buys from someone else).

That's why the greatest experts on sales insist that you must *close the sale*. Yet this phrase—one of the most accepted in business—says all the wrong things. It suggests that the sale is over—closed—once the transaction is completed. It paints this step in the sales cycle as the "scariest" one for the salesperson, since the customer might very well say no. And it implies that closing is largely a matter of manipulation.

Think of one time when you considered buying something, the salesperson tried to close the sale, and you felt annoyed, manipulated, or helpless. Describe that interaction below:

Wouldn't it be great if these sorts of things didn't happen? The fact is: *They don't have to*. In a truly client-focused approach, trickery isn't needed to get that sale. The buyer and seller simply agree that the proposed solution is the right one. It's a triumphant moment, the point at which the seller has so perfectly fashioned a travel solution for the customer, one that so thoroughly fits the client's needs, that he can't possibly say no.

ACHIEVING AGREEMENT: THE STATISTICS

Several studies have shown that when dealing with travel, 20 percent of the sales are closed by the salesperson, 20 percent are closed by the client (without any impetus from the salesperson) and 60 percent are not closed immediately or at all. Another study, however, indicates that 60 percent of those who contact a travel seller are ready to buy. In the space below, write your theory as to why 20 percent change their mind and either don't buy or buy later.

Of course, the recommendation may be perfect, but customers aren't. Travel professionals do benefit from the fact that their clients are usually motivated buyers—it's not like you're selling life insurance, Amway products, or T-shirts. But in the travel business there are customers who can't make a decision, who resist buying quality, and who phone-shop for the best deal. Knowing how to close—to nudge clients toward agreeing to what's best for them (and you)—can certainly help with such buyers.

STALLS AND SCALES

Sometimes salespeople encounter what is called a stall. **A stall occurs when a customer, despite all that you do, seemingly does not wish to purchase right away.** Some examples of stall phrases:

- "I want to think it over."
- "I'm only browsing."
- "That's more than I was thinking of spending."
- "I need to talk to . . ."

A stall doesn't necessarily mean that you have no chance to close the sale then and there. You must "balance the scale." Think of the stall as a weight on one side of a scale. You must counter the stall by placing a benefits recap and perhaps some closing techniques on the other side, enough to make the scale tip in your direction. If your efforts fail, you must encourage the customer to return to you when and if the stall ends. If it's appropriate to your sales situation, you should also perhaps follow up a few days later to find out if the mental conflict your customer had has ended.

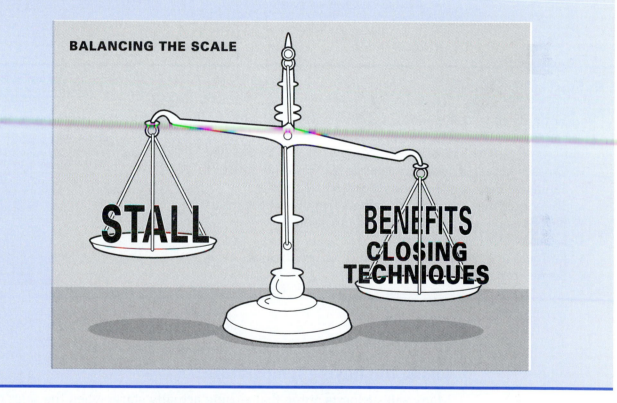

BALANCING THE SCALE

STALL

BENEFITS
CLOSING
TECHNIQUES

Those Agreement Signals

When is the best time to close a sale? At the moment the client decides to buy. But you're not a mind reader. How can you sense when someone is ready to buy? Here are some subtle, telling signals that business-to-business, within-business, and to-the-public sellers look for. Most apply to face-to-face selling, but some are relevant to phone sales, too.

Positive Signs: The customer or client . . .

- Appears to relax his body or voice
- Nods, ever so slightly, to what you say
- Rubs her hands together
- Strokes his chin
- Moves something out of the way from between the two of you (e.g., an object on a desk)
- Increases speech pattern speed
- Touches something directly associated with travel (e.g., the little model airplane or globe on your desk)
- Asks about the price, booking details, payment conditions, cancellation options, etc.
- Says, "Sounds good to me!"
- Consults a calendar or organizer
- Agrees with almost everything you say
- Leans forward
- Puts herself verbally in the travel picture (e.g., "How long is the flight?," "Do I need a passport?")
- Addresses you by name

NEGATIVE SIGNS

You not only have to recognize positive agreement signals; you must spot *negative* ones, too. Here are some: The client . . .

- Crosses his arms or otherwise "closes" his body posture
- Seems restless, shifting body position frequently
- Touches things that have nothing to do with the transaction
- Becomes too quiet (especially on the phone)
- Leans back or slouches
- Reduces eye contact with you and/or briefly looks away
- Seems impatient

Taking the Buying Temperature

Many sales experts argue that closing actually starts when the sales cycle itself begins, that achieving agreement, especially in consultative situations, is built on small steps throughout the process. This makes plenty of sense. It also makes sense to periodically test buyers for interest, to find out if they are moving toward a commitment to buy. Here are some examples of questions that "take the buyer's temperature":

- "How does that sound to you?"
- "Does this fit your plans?"
- "So, what you think of this idea?"

- "How close is that to what you were thinking about?"
- "What do you like most about this option?"
- "Does this sound good to you?"

By encouraging buyers to make little, positive decisions throughout the sales interaction, you're guiding them toward that final agreement to purchase what you're offering. Such questions also help you gauge if you're on the right track. Better to find out if the customer likes each part of your idea before you get too far into the transaction, then have to backtrack and pursue a whole different recommendation avenue.

VIRTUAL CLOSING

Is closing relevant to on-line sales? Yes, but it's not quite as dramatic. When someone buys something on-line, they are, in effect, closing their own sale. Remember, though, that all the marketing that went into convincing that purchaser to buy (including the Web site) represents the closing tactics.

Bear-Trap Closes

A bear trap is a terribly gruesome device. Unlike, say, a tranquilizer dart, it has no concern for the animal. It focuses only on one goal: capture.

Some closing techniques are very much the same. They have no concern for the customer. The only goal is to capture the sale. Unfortunately, salespeople are taught to do these all the time. Here's one example:

"Just sign here and the car will be yours. Unless you do so, though, I can't guarantee this price."

Can you think of two other manipulative closing tactics like this one? Write them here.

1.

2.

Here are four types of bear-trap closes that are common to all sectors of the travel industry, with examples:

- **The scarcity close:** "There are only a few staterooms left . . ."
- **The choice close:** "Would you prefer a regular room or a concierge-level room?" (This, before the customer has even decided to stay at the hotel.)
- **The urgency close:** "This airfare may go up this weekend."
- **The deposit close:** "Just give me your credit card number and I'll hold the reservation for 24 hours. You're under no obligation." (But the customer is indeed forced into some level of commitment.)

What's wrong with these closing techniques?

1. **Consumers recognize them for what they are.** In today's client-focused sales environment and with an increasingly savvy public, techniques like these feel manipulative, presumptuous, and stale. They can erode whatever goodwill was established prior to the close.
2. **They're often dishonest.** Maybe there are *plenty* of staterooms left. Probably the airfare *won't go up*. (If there really are only a few staterooms remaining or the price will likely go up, that's a different matter. The strategy is totally justified.)
3. **They focus totally on making money and not on a customer's needs.** Of course, profit is important. But if it's achieved through trickery, that victory is hollow. Bear-trap techniques don't create a win-win situation, but often an "I win-you lose" scenario instead.

Better Closes

Are some closing techniques more customer-friendly than others? Yes. And many are quite creative, too. Here are twelve that can be useful, especially if the customer goes into a buying stall. Some can only be used in consultative situations, others in transactional ones.

The "You Deserve It" Close   Some people hesitate to buy a vacation—especially if they see it as self-indulgent or too upscale. But they may have worked hard all year to take such a trip. So why not remind them that it's okay to reward themselves (or their family) with that convertible car rental, that hotel suite, or that upscale tour? They've earned it.

The "Smiling" Close   The goal: to get the customer to smile just before asking for the business. If you smile while you talk to someone, that person is likely to mirror your action. In turn, when they smile, it causes the release of naturally occurring, pleasure-provoking chemicals (endorphins) into the bloodstream. Good moods usually bring good results. Smiling people buy.

The "Left Brain to Right Brain" Close   When people plan a trip, they often rely on the logical, reasonable part of their brain. But as we've seen, it's the right brain—the emotional, sensitive, "touchy-feely" part—that goes on vacation. If you sense that over-rationality is getting in the way of the close, begin stressing the emotional payoff that the trip will create. The client's right brain may kick in and get out of that purchasing stall.

MINI ACTIVITY: SELLING TO THE RIGHT BRAIN

For each scenario, come up with a sentence that would appeal to a customer's right brain:

- You think the client should rent a convertible:

- You're convinced a trip to Hawaii would be perfect for them:

- You're sure that an escorted tour would be the right choice for this couple:

The "I'll Throw It In" Close   "If you buy this stereo package, I'll throw in upgraded headphones for free." Heard something like that before? The "I'll throw it in" close is a rare one in front-line travel sales, but it does happen. For example, a travel agent who charges a service fee might waive it. Or he might charge the fee, but "throw in" free travel insurance. (In reality, the service fee offsets the net price of the insurance.) This also works very well in business-to-business selling. A hotel sales representative says that if a tour company agrees, then and there, to the proposed lodging rate, the hotel will provide free continental breakfast to the tour passengers.

MINI ACTIVITY: WHOM DID YOU TRUST?

Try to think of three things you bought in your life because someone recommended them to you. Write those three things below, with the person's name and what relationship he or she has/had with you. (Your best friend, your sister, etc.)

1.

2.

3.

The Testimonial Close   People buy what other people buy. They trust what creates satisfaction for others. How else to explain hotel ratings, "ten best" lists, celebrity spokespersons, and movie reviews? Testimonials work especially well as you approach agreement, but the type you use should depend on the customer's style. Mentioning the experience of other customers works well with sociable people; statistics (e.g., 95 percent of all people who take cruises love them) may convince a more left-brain type; status-conscious individuals often respond to upscale magazine testimonials, like those of *Condé Nast Traveler*.

If you use a testimonial close, though, make sure that what you've recommended matches your customer's needs. You should never recommend something only because someone else recommended it to you.

The "I'm on Your Side" Close   Author Zig Ziglar, who probably is *the* master of closing strategies, cites a cookware salesperson named Merlie Hoke, of Great Fall, South Carolina. As she nears the end of a transaction, she says, "Oh, this is so beautiful! I'm going to help you get it!" This converts quite easily to the travel sales environment—especially when the salesperson is about to check availability of a cruise, hotel room, or other similar, wonderful experience.

The "Try It on For Size" Close   Been to a clothing store? Then you know this one. You try something on, it looks good on you, how can you resist? But is this possible in travel sales? Absolutely. When a cruise line urges you, through an enticing cruise commercial, to try its product, it is, for that brief commercial moment, granting you a virtual, try-it-on-for-size experience. Internet-based virtual reality "tours" of a resort do the same. Face-to-face salespeople can tap these very same resources at a key moment in the sale to help their customers "experience" what they're thinking of buying.

The Assurance Close   If a client sees you as an expert and feels that you really have her needs in mind, all you may have to do is underscore your certainty: "I'm really convinced this package meets your needs. Shall I go ahead and book it for you?" Body language experts also claim that you should "steeple" your hands into an upside-down V shape at this moment. Somehow this symbolically reinforces the accuracy of what you say. (Politicians use this all the time.)

The "Smart Shopper" Close   Compliment the customer on being a "smart shopper"—for doing accurate research or asking the right questions. If they've done all that work, they do indeed deserve praise. And that praise may be all the reinforcement they need to buy from you.

CLOSING FOR EVERYONE

Many people believe that agreement-reaching techniques are valuable only for front-line-to-the-public sales. Nothing could be further from the truth. It's a closing tactic when:

- A tour company sales rep, at the conclusion of her presentation, offers an override to a travel agency if it continues to sell her company's packages in a "preferred" relationship
- An employee justifies his value to a company and asks for a raise
- An airline's direct-mail piece promises extra mileage points for certain flights during a certain period of time
- A convention center offers to provide free meeting rooms if a company stages its trade show there

The Sensory Close   Movie theaters know that the smell of fresh popcorn entices people to buy. So does Mrs. Fields Cookies, whose retail spaces open onto mall traffic without any windows to impede that incredible, seductive cookie aroma. So, too, does Noah's New York Bagels, whose employees sometimes put out little samples for people to taste.

Can appealing to the senses work in travel? Consider one travel agent who, toward the end of a sale, would bring out a bowl of M&M's and offer them to her clients as they contemplated a trip to Walt Disney World; or fine Swiss chocolates to a Europe-bound traveler; or candied tropical fruit slices to someone thinking about a Caribbean holiday. Or how about this: The Hawaii Visitors & Convention Bureau sometimes places a drop of exotic flower essence on each table just before attendees arrive for one of its presentations.

The Mirror Close   An interesting technique to try is to echo the very same phrases and hot-button issues that the client favored during the sales process. If a customer says, "I want a spacious room so we and the kids don't feel crowded," then, just before asking for the business, you emphasize that the all-suite hotel you're recommending has plenty of room and that a sofa bed is in the suite's living room area.

The Agreement Close   Sometimes all it takes to close a sale—especially when you've done an especially perfect job of matching recommendations to client needs—is just to ask for the business. The phrase can be simple.

- "May I book this for you?"
- "All right, shall we do it?"
- "So, I think we're ready to get this going. Okay?"
- "Looks like we've got the best solution to your travel needs."
- "So, does this fit your plans?"
- "I'd be delighted to set this up for you today. Shall we do it?"

A Few Miscellaneous Thoughts on Closing

Achieving agreement is the most rewarding part of the sales cycle. To refine it even more, consider the following:

- **Don't oversell.** If you sense that your client is ready to buy, ask for the business. You may wish to continue to inventory all those wonderful benefits, to do a truly thorough job, but once a customer seems ready, go for it. Anything else will irritate the buyer, waste your time, and perhaps undermine the whole thing.
- **Have faith in what you sell.** Selling without conviction is a counterproductive, demoralizing, and cynical thing to do. Believe what you say, trust what you sell, or find something better to recommend.
- **Be confident.** What sets winning salespeople apart from mediocre ones? Their attitude. If you're confident in your skills, believe in your recommendations, and treat your clients the way you'd treat your best friends, then you're certain to succeed.
- **No closing technique is perfect.** People are different, moods change and some customers can't make a decision. The greatest baseball players hit the ball only 30 percent of the time. If you close more than 40 percent of your sales, you're a champion.

Before finishing, let's see if you can remember the six major steps of sales that constitute the sales cycle. Try to use the terminology that this book recommends. If *necessary*, go back through the text and find the steps you forgot.

1.

2.

3.

4.

5.

6.

These steps aren't written in stone. Different experts label or organize them in different ways. Moreover, this list isn't necessarily comprehensive. Are there any steps you feel we might have missed? If so, write them here:

THE LITTLE STEPS OF SALES

Perhaps you'll encounter the steps you just listed above in this, our final chapter topic. For the sales cycle also embraces many "mini-steps" that tie the entire process together. Often omitted, these minor steps can create a major boost in your ability to sell travel.

Make Small Talk

As you've seen, researchers have discovered something quite interesting: Salespeople who make small talk about *anything except business* before determining needs have a much better chance of coming to an agreement with the buyer. So, after your greeting but before qualifying, talk about weather, family—anything but travel-related issues.

Recap

We've mentioned recapping in Chapter 3. Recapping, or summarizing needs, serves four purposes:

1. It ensures that you correctly understand what the customer needs and wants.
2. It validates to the client that you've listened carefully.
3. It forces you to actually pay attention, since you know you'll have to repeat what the customer has said.
4. It establishes you as a genuine professional.

In the travel sales process, you should recap *twice*: after the qualifying stage ("So you've said that you'd like an afternoon flight," etc.) and again just after you've presented your recommendation ("So I'd recommend the Marriott Marquis on Times Square, since you want to stay close to the Theater District," etc.). Note that in the second recap, you link your advice to the client's need and describe the benefit. This makes the recap that much more persuasive.

See Them Off

No, you don't have to go with them to the airport. But you should *see them off from the sales experience* you've both been through. How can you do this?

- Verbalize your excitement about the travel experience they're about to have.
- Ask if there's anything else you can do for them.
- If appropriate, express the hope that you'll see or hear from them when they return.
- Thank them for their business.
- Wish them a wonderful trip.

Follow Up

Here's one of the most common forms of follow-up. A hotel leaves a survey in each room for the guest to fill out, then the guests rate each aspect of their stay. The hotel and, if applicable, its chain analyze the results and use them to refine the experience they offer. Indeed, some of the keenest insights any business can attain come through such customer feedback. (It's called *managing after-sales satisfaction*.)

Dealing with complaints is another form of follow-up. More about that in our next chapter.

Follow-up is often considered a step of *marketing*. It can, however, be very much a part of the sales model itself. When it is, it becomes a fiercely powerful way to generate customer loyalty. Some experts, in fact, include it as one of the *major* steps of the sales process.

Here's an example: When Mazda began selling automobiles in the United States, it would regularly contact its customers about a month after they had bought their cars. Mazda would ask if they could send someone to the buyer's home, no less, to find out how pleased they were with their new car. During the visit, the Mazda representative would thank the person for their purchase, find out if anything needed fixing (and set up an appointment with the service department for them), ask a series of satisfaction questions (the answers would direct subsequent marketing decisions) and present the customer with a small gift. Impressive, don't you think?

Here's another example. A couple books a Tauck escorted tour to Hawaii. Before the clients leave on their trip, Tauck sends them a complimentary copy of James Michener's novel *Hawaii*. When they return, a bouquet of tropical flowers awaits.

Have you encountered an especially impactful follow-up gesture? It can be either travel-related or not. Describe it here:

Here are some other follow-up gestures that travel providers have actually used. They represent a wide spectrum of situations. Perhaps one is similar to what you wrote above:

- A room service employee calls an hour after a meal was delivered to find out if the guest enjoyed the meal.
- An airline that canceled its only flight from Los Angeles to Honolulu that day—delaying the customer's holiday for twenty-four hours (making for a shorter vacation)—sends that customer a free ticket to anywhere in the United States. (Yes, it happens.)
- An attraction sends a gift to the itinerary planner of a major tour operator that has brought considerable business during the recently finished tourist season.
- An auto rental representative leaves a message at a client's hotel, expressing the hope that all has gone well with the customer's driving experience.
- The sales director at an incentive company follows up internally with the company's operations team to find out how a certain trip went.
- A travel agent orders a bottle of champagne for a couple. It awaits them in their stateroom with a note saying, "Have a great cruise!"

As you can imagine, though, follow-up gestures require not just thoughtfulness, but also time, money, creativity, and perhaps extra staffing. Is it worth it? Consider the following. Depending on the context, follow-up can:

- Personalize the sales process well past the customer's expectations
- Provide critical feedback—both positive and negative
- Strongly cement the buyer-seller relationship
- Defuse client frustration with a problem and perhaps lay the path for a solution
- Establish the seller as a conscientious and caring person
- Set the stage, perhaps, for a future sale

Worth it, don't you think?

MINI ACTIVITY: FOLLOW-UP

Why does follow-up happen so rarely? The three most cited reasons:

1. We're too busy to do it.

2. It's a cost we can't afford.

3. We might find out something went wrong.

Write what you might say to overcome each of these three objections:

1.

2.

3.

Follow-Up Thoughts on Follow-Up   Here are a few things to keep in mind about follow-up:

- **Follow-up can occur at many points in relation to the trip.** Before, during, after, even long after—all these are suitable points for follow-up.
- **The cost of the follow-up should be commensurate with the profit.** An expensive travel purchase warrants a grand gesture, a smaller one something less expensive. Remember, though: *Creative* follow-up, even if it costs almost nothing or is free (an e-mail wish for a successful trip with some sort of clever animation), can make a major impression.
- **Follow-up should not compete with other things for attention.** Many companies send Christmas cards to clients. A flood of competing cards, though, drains the gesture of its impact. But a birthday card, Thanksgiving card, or anniversary message? Now those are different.

Name: _____   Date: _____

ACTIVITY #1   IF I WERE YOU . . .

Imagine that you are a travel agent in Atlanta. A couple has come to you to plan their first vacation ever to New York City. They tell you they have a very wide range of interests and like to do all sorts of activities during a trip.

You arrange their flights and hotel. What *eight* specific things might you consider offering them to enhance their trip? Write them below. (You may use any resources at your disposal to research the possibilities.)

1.

2.

3.

4.

5.

6.

7.

8.

What resources did you use to come up with these options?

Name: _____   Date: _____

ACTIVITY #2   FOLLOW UP ON FOLLOW-UP

Interview several people to find out what follow-up gesture, because of its creativity and/or impact, impressed them. They can be travel or nontravel related. You may also list other instances of follow-up that happened to you. Come up with at least five examples.

1.

2.

3.

4.

5.

Of the nontravel examples you listed above, which ones would be "translatable" to the travel environment, and why?

5

Serving the Travel Customer

OBJECTIVES

After reading this chapter, you'll be able to:

- Define service and its vocabulary

- Explain why service is eroding

- Practice the fifteen standards of service excellence

- Effectively deal with complaints

There's good news and bad news about this chapter. The good news: You're about to receive one of the most precious things in our society: insight into how to treat customers well. The bad news: More and more, you'll notice how poorly *you're treated* when you're shopping, buying, and interacting with people who are supposed to be attending to *your* needs.

It's easy to conclude that the ability to deliver great service is just a matter of personality. Some people are naturally thoughtful, gracious, and polite. Others are quite the opposite. Yet how can you explain that there are *entire companies* that are known for delivering superior service, while others are notorious for their indifference? Is it just a matter of hiring the right people? Perhaps. But the main source of consistently good service is a corporation's culture, the philosophy it communicates to its employees and the training that it provides.

Let's do a little exercise. Identify a company—either travel related or not—that you feel renders superior service. Then give three reasons why you chose that company:

Company: _____

1.

2.

3.

By completing this exercise, you've probably pinpointed some of the very same service strategies you'll soon learn in this chapter.

Now another exercise. Identify a company—travel related or not—that you feel delivers *poor* service. Give three reasons for your conclusion:

Company: _____

1.

2.

3.

You now have a list of what *not* to do to customers, or at least what bothers you the most about lackluster service.

Almost surely you felt some sharp emotions as you identified each company and compiled your reasons. That's why service is so important. Done well, it can make the buying experience an emotionally happy one, one that's worth repeating. Poor service, on the other hand, irritates customers and makes them want to buy somewhere else.

Customer service is especially crucial to the travel industry, since positive experiences are the ultimate goal of all travel. Travelers want more than a nice hotel room, flight, or rental car: *They want to be treated well.*

HOW SERVICE IS MEASURED

Companies assess the service they deliver in a number of ways. *Customer surveys* are perhaps the most popular. They often consist of a printed form or **"comment card"** that you fill out, in effect "grading" all aspects of service. You then mail it in or drop it off for analysis. Companies also sometimes interview random customers orally, one-on-one, either in person or over the phone. This approach works well, because it elicits more detailed feedback and is based on an unbiased cross-section. (With printed surveys, dissatisfied customers are more likely than satisfied ones to respond, thus skewing the results.)

A second source of service analysis is the focus group. **A focus group is a group of people, chosen either randomly or in a targeted manner, who, under the guidance of a trained moderator, express their opinions on a service or product.** Usually composed of twelve people or less, a focus group enables a company to go beyond the narrow categories and questions of a customer survey. The moderator asks questions that are open-ended and that yield rich results. The group is often observed through a one-way mirror and/or videotaped. This permits easier analysis and usually leads to a summarizing follow-up report for management to review.

A third way to evaluate service is through a **mystery shopper.** Here's how it works: A person hired by a company but unknown to that company's service staff calls or visits the organization's places of business. The mystery shopper pretends to be a regular customer and observes and later reports on how the employees react to certain predetermined requests. The mystery shopper technique is very effective, since it permits analysis of normal, everyday service performance.

WHY SERVICE EXCELLENCE IS SO IMPORTANT

Most successful companies place great emphasis on service excellence. They already understand that good service:

- Builds loyal customers and attracts new ones

- Leads to strong word-of-mouth about their business
- Reduces the level of complaints
- Reinforces workforce efficiency and satisfaction
- Adds value to whatever they provide and often justifies charging somewhat higher prices—many people are willing to pay more for a pleasant buying experience

They also know that more and more people have now experienced great service, the kind you get at, say, Disneyland. To cite a cliché: the service performance bar has been raised.

Look back on the company you listed as a positive role model for service. Does it charge a bit more than its competitors do? And what of the negative example? Is it a company that relies on low prices? Remember: *Cheaper* has two meanings: less expensive and of poorer quality. Yes, a company that sells travel commodities to the very price-sensitive can perhaps afford to skimp on service. But unless they sell vast quantities of products, it will be difficult for them to make money.

This leads to another, related conclusion: In travel, *companies that sell commodity-like products are usually perceived as providing poorer service than those that sell experiential ones.* Airlines and car rental firms, for instance, are not generally known for great service. Cruise lines and tour operators are.

Ironically, though, consumers do expect flight attendants, car rental service representatives, and airline gate agents to treat them every bit as well as a tour manager or stateroom steward would. This circles back to our left brain-right brain theory from Chapter 4: People may buy with their left brain, *but it's the right brain that goes on vacation.* Logical, left-brain thinking may drive buyers to the lowest price. Once they're experiencing what they bought, though, they seem to forget the fact that strong cost savings often lead to weak service. The right brain doesn't care. It just wants to feel good.

The WIIFMs of Service

Service excellence has a clear value to both consumers and businesses. But how about *those who deliver that service?* What's in it for them? (Or as some abbreviate it, what's their WIIFM—**What's In It For Me?**)

Try to list three ways in which knowing how to provide great service is good for *the employee.*

1.

2.

3.

Compare what you listed above with the following reasons for a person to render fine service: It helps build personal pride. It generates positive feedback from customers. It reinforces job security and makes advancement more likely. It often diminishes on-the-job stress. It can make the job more fun. The best reason to give good service: It makes you feel better.

Remember, too, that service skills are useful not only to front-liners, but also to people at all levels of a company. As with selling, service happens between businesses and within businesses, too.

WHY SERVICE IS ERODING

Jay Leno tells the story of a service experience he once had. Used to being recognized, he was dismayed that a supermarket checkout clerk not only failed to acknowledge him, but said nothing to him after he handed over his money. "Not even a 'thank you'?" he asked. Her response: "It's printed on your receipt."

Most people feel that, over the past few decades, service in North America has deteriorated badly. What are the reasons? Here are five:

1. Increased work stress has made it more difficult for people to be nice to others while on the job.
2. Today's preoccupation with technology has shifted the focus away from people skills.
3. The desire to streamline operations and reduce costs often subverts patient, thorough service.
4. Service training often takes a back seat to logistic and sales training. (One study concluded that the typical business spends less than $3 per employee yearly on service training.)
5. Society itself has devalued good manners. We're in an age when "in your face," "talk to the hand," and "whatever" are favored phrases. It's not surprising that a University of Michigan study discovered that 71 percent of over 1,000 federal court employees claim to have experienced serious rudeness at work within a five-year period. If anything,

that statistic seems surprisingly low. Almost surely, today's "manners meltdown" has strongly contributed to the worsening of service.

Do you have any other theories for why good service has waned? Write them here:

VIRTUAL SERVICE

As travel-related companies struggle to find, train, and keep good servicepeople, they have turned to technology and automation to deliver nonpersonal, "virtual" service. (Cost savings are usually a motive, too.) At airports, kiosks swiftly furnish customers with e-tickets and boarding passes. In hotels, automated systems provide ever-friendly wake-up calls. On their phone reservation lines, tour companies present a series of "press one for . . . press two for . . ." options to respond to callers' needs.

Of course, *self-service* has been around a long time, in all businesses. When it leads to complicated routines, wasted time and unresolvable problems, however, self-service irritates the customer and leads to that familiar refrain, "Isn't there anyone who can help me?" That assumes, of course, that the somebody will turn out to be a helpful, responsive, informed, and caring person.

Virtual service, when correctly conceived, may—in some situations—work. Witness the Internet. The greatest threat, however, is *system failure:* a booking gets lost, the computer is down, the directions are unclear. Such system failures affect personal service, too. But people tend to figure out ways to serve customers, even when the system doesn't work.

THE IDEAL SERVICE PROVIDER

We all have our ideas of what a great serviceperson is like. Read the following list of twenty-five adjectives that might describe that ideal person:

accurate	energetic	patient	respectful	understanding
alert	enthusiastic	pleasant	sensitive	upbeat
anticipatory	flexible	positive	sincere	welcoming
appreciative	friendly	proud	supportive	well-groomed
cheerful	helpful	reliable	thoughtful	well-spoken

Now choose the *two* you feel are the most important to service success:

What do you think the two adjectives you chose say *about you*? Write your response here:

Your two adjectives—and the reasons behind them—are almost surely different from what someone else might choose. This shows that a skilled serviceperson must develop and practice a broad, diversified range of personality traits to be successful.

Achieving service excellence is an intriguing challenge. Once mastered, it sets you apart in a dramatic and impressive way. It's not surprising that many travel industry leaders started as front-line servicepeople. And it's no wonder that certain servicepeople, like tour managers and waiters, get great tips when they do their jobs right and well.

Internal Contracts

In Chapter 1 you learned a definition of what service is. Can you recall it? Write it, as best you can remember, here:

Now go back to page 4 and compare what you just wrote with our "official" definition. The way a person should treat customers is often defined quite specifically by a company. This is sometimes referred to as an **internal contract,** because it implies an agreement between the employer and employee. That internal contract is, in a sense, an external one too, since it affects how you treat people outside your corporate culture.

Some examples of possible internal contract expectations:

- When not on the microphone, a tour guide should stroll through the motorcoach to make sure everything is fine with the passengers.
- A travel agent should answer the phone within three rings.

- A cruise line stateroom steward must make up the stateroom within two hours of the guest's departure from that room.
- A reservationist should always use an official four-part greeting.
- A hotel front entrance valet must welcome a guest driving up in a car within 30 seconds of arrival and offer to unload the luggage.
- A theme park employee should always help guests embark and disembark from a ride.

Note that almost all these service performance standards have one thing in common: They're *measurable*. This enables the employer to statistically rate service—and individual—efficiency.

Measurable service expectations, however, cannot gauge *how* the service was performed. A reservationist can deliver the official four-part greeting in a spiritless, indifferent and/or muddled manner. The *quality* of service delivery—though hard to measure—makes a world of difference to customers.

SERVICE GAPS AND CULTURE

Experts often talk of **service gaps, areas where performance doesn't match what is expected.** Author Leonard Berry identifies five major service gaps that managers are likely to encounter:

1. Between what customers expect and what you think they expect
2. Between customer-focus standards and your standards
3. Between what your people do and what you want them to do
4. Between what you promise and what you deliver
5. Between what your customers expect and what they experience

Such service expectations, however, vary from culture to culture. The cultural dissonance discussed in Chapter 2 plays a part in service, as well. For example, in Japan, service expectations are very high, higher than those in the United States. Service personnel are exceptionally courteous, respond swiftly to a customer's needs, and are prepared to go well out of their way to keep buyers happy. Japanese visitors to the United States often feel that Americans aren't as polite as they expected. And Americans who travel to developing countries tend to find service gaps common.

THE STANDARDS OF SERVICE EXCELLENCE

Travel-related industries seem to have settled on a distinct set of "best practices" for delivering superior service. As you'll see, they apply to many other businesses, too, and overlap some of the sales strategies you learned earlier. Here they are:

1. **Acknowledge every customer as soon as possible.** Did you ever walk into a hotel and have no one at the front desk notice you were there? They're busy, the phone is ringing, but it doesn't matter: *A serviceperson has no excuse not to recognize that someone needs their assistance.* If that serviceperson is truly occupied with something important, he

should look at the customer, smile and say, "I'll be right with you." To do otherwise is to convey the message: "You're not important. You're just something I process."

This applies to phone service, too. The equivalent proper behavior would be to answer that phone within three rings and, if busy, ask permission from the caller to put her on hold. (Of course, you must return to that call as soon as feasible.) If the situation causes a delay, make sure to apologize. It's a thoughtful gesture that customers appreciate.

2. **Give a warm and sincere greeting.** One seminar presenter describes entering a fast-food restaurant. No other customers were there. The person working the counter, his eyes glazed over, called out, "May I help the next customer?"

   Greetings—in person or on the phone—should not seem automatic or mindless. They must, instead, project friendliness, dedication, and a genuine desire to help. A cheery energy should continue past that welcome through the entire interaction with the customer.

3. **Discover and use the person's name.** Angela Lehrke is a shore excursion director with Peter Deilmann Cruises. Each week she greets 200 people as they check in to her ship. At that point she memorizes their names. All 200. Every week. Her astonishing feat underscores a more modest lesson: Using a person's name works equally well with service as with sales.

4. **Avoid the forbidden phrases.** Certain words and phrases are terribly counterproductive to good service. The most famous: "It's not my job."

On the next page are some others. Guess how a client might negatively interpret each phrase. We've given you two examples to get you started:

Phrase	*How a customer might interpret it*
1. "I don't know"	*This serviceperson is either lazy or uninformed*
2. "We're really busy"	*I'm not very important to them, I guess*
3. "That's not my department"	
4. "You should have . . ."	
5. "I'll try to . . ."	
6. "You need to . . ."	
7. There's nothing I can do"	
8. "It's company policy"	

Many other phrases defeat service—they're usually synonymous with the above. Some examples:

"I'm not sure"	"You can't"
"You have to . . ."	"You should . . ."
"Would you mind . . ."	"I'm not sure why"
"I can't"	"I want you to . . ."

So how do you get around such unhelpful language? Here are seven ways:

1. Use positive, not negative language.
2. If you need to ask someone to do something, say, "Will you . . . ," "Could you . . . ," or "You can . . . ,"
3. Start your sentence with "I will . . ." Take responsibility.
4. Avoid starting your response with *but*. It immediately sounds like you're about to say something negative.
5. Start with "What I will do for you is . . ." This works especially well with complaints.
6. Give the reason for your response first and paint it *as a benefit to the customer*. This will help soften whatever you say afterwards. For example: "To help you save time when you call in the future, could you note this confirmation number?"
7. Always say "thank you" when someone does something nice for you, and "you're welcome" when someone says "thank you" to you.

EFFECTIVE SERVICE VOCABULARY

These words and phrases work especially well in the service situation:

"How may I help you?"	"Let me find out for you."
"How can it be corrected?"	"Here are some options . . ."
"What have you considered?"	"I understand your concern."
"Which do you prefer?"	Will/willing
"What are the alternatives?"	Able
"What are the options?"	"I apologize for . . ."
"What would you like me to do?"	"I made a mistake."
"I understand."	"Here's what I can do for you."

5. **Pay extra attention to "moments of truth."** Jan Carlzon, former president of SAS Airlines, coined the oft-repeated phrase **moments of truth** to describe those **key moments when a customer is most likely to make a decision about a serviceperson and the company he or she represents.** Among the most obvious moment-of-truth situations:
   - The first few seconds of interaction between a client and a serviceperson
   - When a serviceperson first responds to a request or complaint
   - When something goes from being in doubt to its resolution
   - At the very end of a service interaction

   Here's an example. America West Airlines taught its gate agents to say the following when a passenger cleared a waitlist for a flight: "I'm so glad, Mr. (or Ms.) —, that we were able to get you on this flight." That's so much better than the usual: "Here's your boarding card."

6. **Manage your personal "packaging."** Appearance, the neatness of your workspace, what you wear, the professionalism of your writing—all these and more make up the "package" that customers perceive as they interact with you. Remember: They judge the entire organization by the image you project.

7. **Remember "you're always on stage."** Disney calls its employees "cast members." That label implies that you must be, in a sense, like a good actor and project the role of service—no matter what mood you're in or even what personality you usually have.

THE RITZ-CARLTON CREDO

Ritz-Carlton has long been known as a provider of superior service. Here are some of the things Ritz-Carlton tells every employee in its "credo":

- Use the guest name, if and when possible.
- Anticipate and comply with guest needs.
- Consider yourself "ladies and gentlemen serving ladies and gentlemen."
- Always maintain positive eye contact.
- Smile—we are always "on stage."
- Maintain uncompromising levels of cleanliness.
- Practice teamwork and lateral service.
- Be an ambassador of your hotel both in and outside of the workplace.
- Respond to requests with the phrase, "My pleasure."
- Any employee who receives a guest complaint "owns" it.
- Respond to guest wishes within ten minutes of the request.
- Follow up with a telephone call within twenty minutes.
- Escort guests, rather than pointing out directions to another area of the hotel.
- Eliminate call transfers whenever possible.

Ritz-Carlton employee at elevators.
(Courtesy of Ritz-Carlton, Boston)

8. **Deliver what your company promises.** It's always important to keep up on your company's expectations and, more importantly, on what *the customer expects*. The best source for these expectations may not be company memos, though. It's that company's advertising. For example, Norwegian Cruise Lines "Freestyle" and Princess Cruises "Choice" campaigns implied that guests would have great freedom while onboard their cruise vessels. This meant, among other things, that employees had to be especially flexible with customer requests and avoid the "regimentation" kind of thinking that had long characterized much of the cruise business.

   This also implies that you must *do what you promise*. If you said you'd deliver a package to a guest's room within fifteen minutes, you must do so (or don't make that promise). If you're a travel agent and assured your client you'd call with information within twenty-four hours but actually called three days later, your reason won't matter. The client has probably gone to someone else more punctual to book their trip.

9. **Exceed expectations.** This phrase has become somewhat of a cliché—perhaps because so many companies fail in their promise to excel. Whatever the exhortation—go the extra mile, dazzle them with service—the meaning is this: you should do *more* than your customer expects. An extra attraction not on the tour itinerary, complimentary fruit in a bowl at the hotel's front desk, free home delivery of cruise documents by a travel agency to a client who's especially busy—these are the kinds of gestures that loom large in a customer's perception of a company's devotion to service.

   Remember, though, that expectations vary according to that company's consumer image. What guests expect from a Motel 6 is very different from what they anticipate from a Four Seasons.

VALUE LEVELS

The value levels of various travel suppliers help shape customer service expectations. Here are some examples of different "tiers" of travel products. (Note: Individual examples from each value category may be higher or lower than indicated. Also, brand quality differences exist within categories.)

Value level	Hotel chains	Escorted tour operators	Cruise lines
Budget	Motel 6 Super 8	N/A	N/A
Economy	Days Inn Hampton Inns Ramada	Collette Contiki Cosmos	American Canadian Caribbean Regal
Mid-level	Doubletree Hilton Holiday Inn Hyatt Radisson Sheraton	Brendan Brennan Globus Mayflower Perillo Trafalgar Westours	Carnival Norwegian Orient Royal Caribbean
Premium	Fairmont Marriott Renaissance Westin	Japan and Orient Tours Maupintour Tauck	Celebrity Cunard Crystal Disney Holland America Princess Radisson Seven Seas
Luxury	Four Seasons Peninsula Ritz-Carlton	Abercrombie & Kent Intrav Travcoa	Seabourn Silversea

10. **Anticipate customer needs.** Skilled servicepeople don't simply react to customer requests. They proactively look for opportunities to serve those customers' needs. One example: If you're having a soft drink at a restaurant, isn't it nice when the server offers to refill your glass when it's low, without you having to ask? Or if you were on a cruise, wouldn't it be great if—after you return from a swim to your poolside chair—your towel had been replaced with a clean, dry one? How about when you call an airline to make a reservation: Wouldn't it be helpful if the reservationist offers you seat selection, even if you didn't think of asking about it?

CUSTOMER RETENTION

It's a well-known statistic: The average company loses 10 to 30 percent of its customers each year. Many reasons account for this loss. Here are the six most common. After reading all of them, check the box of the one you think accounts for the *greatest* loss of customers.

❑ The customer moves to a new neighborhood.
❑ The prices are perceived as too high.
❑ The customer dies.
❑ The customer senses the sales/serviceperson is indifferent.
❑ The customer is dissatisfied with the product or service.
❑ The customer had a good relationship with the sales/serviceperson, who then leaves the company.

The answer, according the White House Office of Consumer Affairs: salesperson indifference. In fact, 68 percent of those surveyed said that indifference was their main motive for leaving. (The others: 14 percent product/service dissatisfaction; 9 percent price; 5 percent loss of good relationship; 3 percent moved; 1 percent died.)

Businesses clearly see that if they improve their employees' attitudes toward service, they will have addressed over two-thirds of their customer loss. A program that seeks to do this is often called a **customer retention program.**

Another way to anticipate needs is to identify problems and solve them *before they occur.* If a convention center employee sees that a lightbulb is burned out over a speaker's podium, he won't wait until the speaker complains. He'll solve the problem then and there. If a travel agent realizes that she has only one or two brochures of a certain tour operator left, she'll order more before the agency runs out. If a hotel front desk manager notices that people are waiting too long at the front desk, he should not only pitch in to help, but later suggest to the general manager that staffing might be increased during certain hours.

Employees at all levels of a company always should be on the look-out for service gaps, as well as for ways to plan these customer service problems out of the system.

11. **Avoid criticizing.** A famous British TV sketch from the 1970s has a person going to a store's "complaint department" and gently suggesting that he needed to speak to someone about a problem. The head of the complaint department immediately launches into a tirade about *his* problems!

This wonderful sketch underscores the fact that we don't go to someone to hear their complaints. We go to express ours. That's why a number of the strategies we've examined encourage keeping things positive. You should never complain to customers about the product you represent, the company you work for (and its policies), companies that compete with yours, and other customers you've served. You shouldn't whitewash things, of course. Honesty is still the best policy. But servicepeople who complain, blame, or malign are usually perceived by the public as untrustworthy.

12. **Apply lateral service.** Have you noticed that at some airlines, ground crew help check in people when the gate agents are overworked? Or that maintenance staff offer to help "lost" guests at theme parks or resorts? **Lateral service is when people go beyond their job description to help out service workers in other "departments."** It promotes efficient operations, breaks the boredom that comes with routines, encourages **cross-training (acquiring skills in several jobs),** and fortifies team spirit among employees.

13. **Listen and watch carefully**. A key to fulfilling client service needs is to listen to customers very carefully. The same listening tactics you learned in Chapter 2 apply here. Remember: Though hearing happens automatically, listening takes concentration. In face-to-face interactions, you should also pay attention to non-verbal body language to extract clues to the customer's feelings.

14. **Offer a fond farewell**. The words used at the end of the service experience are as important as those at the beginning. A travel agent can leave a voice-mail message wishing the client a great trip. Hotel, cruise line, rail, or theme park employees can express the hope that they'll see the guest again. Such little gestures generate a profound impact—and require so little energy.

15. **Follow up.** Yes, here it is again. The same thing that works for sales applies to service.

Perhaps the most venerable, famous, and persuasive advice of all, however, is this: Do unto others as you would have them do unto you.

HOW MANAGEMENT SHOULD ENCOURAGE SERVICE

In his book *The Service Edge*, Ron Zemke gives eight ways for supervisors and managers to encourage service excellence:

1. Define your objectives in customer-oriented terms.
2. Lead by your example.
3. Develop specific, customer-focused standards.
4. Provide meaningful rewards for service achievements.
5. Involve employees in service planning and new-hire selection.
6. Keep communication clear and constant.
7. Reward teams as well as (and more than) individuals.
8. Manage recognition—and performance—for the long term.

Training Servicepeople

How can supervisory and managerial personnel help ensure that servicepeople will actually do what's expected of them? The answer: through consistent and effective training:

1. **Training must underscore the WIIFMs.** A serviceperson must understand in what way good service will make his or her life easier.
2. **Expected behavior must be made clear.** It's not enough to give vague advice. Training standards must be very precise. "Answering the phone within three rings" is more effective (and measurable) than "Answer the phone promptly." If performance can be measured, it's easier to analyze and shape.
3. **Hold them accountable.** There should be a clear expectation that *consistently* good service (or deficient service) will be noted and acted upon.
4. **Show what good service is.** Observing someone at work who does things right or even just watching a video with people who act out proper service (or even bad service) gives trainees role models on which to base their behavior.
5. **Observe them in action.** Ever call a company and hear the message: "This call may be monitored for quality assurance?" Random performance checks are critical to any phone service environment. Doing this in "live" situations (e.g., at a car rental counter) is more difficult—but it can be done.
6. **Praise and reward excellent behavior.** People love positive feedback but wither in environments where criticism alone comes their way. Positive reinforcement and recognition for superior work are powerful tools. Use them.
7. **Training must be ongoing.** Managers should, on a regular basis, provide fresh guidance on what will please clients and help make them customers for life.

GRAPPLING WITH GRIPES

In the past month, have you had to complain about service you received or something you bought? Describe the situation below, along with the outcome.

You may have struggled with this exercise a bit, since we all tend to erase unpleasant experiences from our memories. This is tightly linked to something psychologists call avoidance behavior.

Avoidance behavior is the *last thing* a business wants. Why? Because it means that the customer will avoid ever doing business again with that company. This explains a widely accepted statistic: Four out of five people who have a complaint don't complain. They simply don't return to the company they have the complaint with.

The White House Office of Consumer Affairs has delved into this even further. Its study produced even more dramatic results: Only 4 percent of dissatisfied customers actually complain. Even worse, these customers tell about ten others of their bad service experience, each of whom, in turn, tells six. That's sixty people. Poor service and other problems get communicated fast—and to a lot of people.

But there's a sunny side to this study. Ninety-five percent of those surveyed said that if their problems were addressed, they would resume business with that company. So how should you deal with complaints? Read on.

WHAT DISSATISFIES CUSTOMERS?

Here, in no particular order, are some of the most common sources of complaints:

- Delays and long waits for service
- Inferior products and services
- Misinformation (verbal or written)
- Procedural mistakes that affect the client
- Conflicting information
- Rude or inefficient service
- Promises made but not delivered
- Refusing to take responsibility for the problem
- Employee dishonesty or lack of integrity
- Manipulation of the customer by employees
- Being told that they were misinformed, wrong, or unimportant
- Slow, complicated or nonexistent problem resolution

Recovery

Most companies describe the process of dealing with dissatisfaction and complaints as **recovery.** What do you think are the keys to successful recovery? Without reading any further, jot down a few ideas here:

Now let's look at the steps that you should take to deal with a complaint. Compare them with what you wrote above.

1. **Fix the customer, not the problem.** What went wrong isn't your primary challenge. It's *the emotions* that the problem triggered. Respect

your clients' feelings and try to soothe them with your words and attitudes.

2. **Don't blame yourself.** Almost surely you weren't the cause of the problem. So don't take it personally. However, *do* take responsibility for correcting the problem, even though it wasn't your fault. (Note: Don't blame the customer, either.)

3. **Let the customer talk.** Consider the last time you had a complaint. Did you plan out in advance what you were going to say? Probably. Your customers do the same. Allow them to present their complaint without interrupting. Remain calm. Listen. Don't let their emotions ignite yours. And even if their complaint is petty or ludicrous, treat it seriously, because, no matter what you may think, it's an important issue to them.

4. **Acknowledge their feelings.** Say that you understand their feelings. Empathize. Important point: It's not necessary to agree with the core of their complaint. It might even be unwise, in case legal action follows. Just agree with their feelings.

5. **Express your regret.** Apologize, even if it's not your fault. Tell them you're sorry for what happened to them.

6. **Suppress explanations or excuses.** Sure, you'd like to describe, clearly and logically, why things went wrong. But the customer is operating on an emotional level—at this stage *logic is largely irrelevant*. Clarifications might be appropriate later, when their anger has abated. But not now, unless they insist on an explanation.

7. **Ask for clarification.** Once the customer becomes less upset, accumulate whatever information you need to devise a solution. Write down the details, if necessary.

8. **Repeat the specifics.** As with sales, you should recap all the details to verify that you've understood the problem correctly and to show that you've been paying attention.

9. **Agree on a plan.** Suggest a solution that you feel addresses the client's dissatisfaction. If they seem unsatisfied with your solution, ask them what it would take to make them happy. If their solution is reasonable, pursue it. If not, suggest an alternative compromise or get one from your immediate supervisor.

10. **Thank the customer.** Explain that you welcome the opportunity to correct a problem—100 percent satisfaction is your company's goal and yours, too. By bringing this issue to your attention, they've helped you achieve that.

11. **See them off.** This, of course, works only in person. But customers usually like to deliver their complaints in person, if they can. Underscore your commitment by walking the client to the door when they leave.

12. **Follow through and follow up.** Take action on the issue as quickly as you can. If you can handle it while the customer is there, do so. If not, follow up later to let the person know how things have been resolved.

One seminar presenter refers to recovery as "turning oops into opportunity." Yes, you can learn from complaints. The most legitimate ones help you refine your delivery of service and understand your customers' buying and service experiences.

99.9 PERCENT

What should a company strive for as a target for service performance? An 80 percent success rate? 90 percent? Would 99.9 percent be unreasonably high?

Consider this: If 99.9 percent were good enough then, in the United States and Canada . . .

- Thirteen newborns would be given to the wrong parents daily
- 130,000 mismatched shoes would be shipped yearly
- Two million documents would be lost by the IRS yearly (but not one would be your tax return)
- 158 million cans of soft drinks produced yearly would be flat
- Three thousand copies of tomorrow's *Wall Street Journal* would be missing a section
- Thirteen flights would crash daily

MAINTAINING SUPERIOR SERVICE

When you're stressed, what do you notice about your behavior? Check each one that happens to you:

- ❏ You feel less energy
- ❏ Your productivity goes down
- ❏ You notice more aches and pains
- ❏ Your interest in things drops
- ❏ You get upset more easily
- ❏ You complain a lot
- ❏ You talk to others less
- ❏ Your concentration decreases
- ❏ You're more frequently late for work
- ❏ You have trouble sleeping or sleep too much
- ❏ You gain, or lose, a lot of weight
- ❏ You're bothered by people who seem happy

If the stress comes from work, that's even more dangerous. Stress can decrease your desire to sell and serve the traveling public. If it goes on too long, job burnout is almost inevitable.

What exacerbates burnout? Handling too many problems. Getting no positive feedback. Having unclear directions. Being assigned too much work.

Providing service itself takes its toll. That's why service is *emotional labor*. It can be just as draining as building a wall, cleaning a house, or driving a truck.

Sometimes dealing with people for hours on end leads to what's called **contact overload.** Many companies deal with this by providing their servicepeople with numerous breaks or by rotating employees to different functions throughout the day. Disney has a novel way of addressing contact overload: It provides a "green space" where service employees can go to relax and regroup.

So be vigilant for any of the behaviors that may subvert your work. Burnout may be just around the corner.

How can you head it off? Here are some strategies the experts recommend:

- Do things that make you happy. Write one example here from your own life:

- Exercise regularly. Cite the one type of exercise you should be doing more:

- Create a measurable work and/or personal goal. What might that be for you?

- Take something that's been bothering you and express it to someone. If that someone is a fellow worker or your boss, be especially diplomatic about it. Is there something like that right now in your life? If so, write it here:

The Circle Effect

A circle effect occurs when an *entire* organization and its customers take on a certain attitude. A positive circle effect, of course, is best. The right corporation chemistry leads to happy employees, who in turn make customers happy, who in turn reinforce the employees' positive attitude.

A negative circle effect, however, is dangerous. A company begins to burn out, with good, caring service yielding to indifferent, overbearing, or semihostile "service" behavior. This is most especially seen in businesses where the customer has no other choice but to patronize that business. The classic example: a state department of motor vehicles. After all, where else can you go?

In such situations, a negative circle effect takes over. Servicepeople treat customers as things to be processed. The customers become irritated, which in turn annoys the employees, who develop animosity toward the people they're supposed to serve, who become angry . . . you get the picture.

Does a negative circle effect ever arise in travel-related businesses? It can, and there's one classic example: the airline industry. "Air rage" results, in part, from staff who process people like so much cargo. After all, if travelers have to get somewhere fast, where else can they go? The effect is made worse by the confined seating in today's aircraft. Confine any animal with too many others of its kind in a small space and strife is sure to result. Customers behave boorishly, which makes flight or gate attendants more angry, which leads to . . . well, you know the results.

It's not easy to counter a negative circle effect, but it can be done. Proper training and a well-conceived rewards system go a long way toward solving the problem.

IN CONCLUSION

Providing great service is a powerful way to connect with your customers, plus it's one of the most sensitive and selfless things you can do for someone. Moreover, it often requires only little things to achieve a huge effect.

When achieved consistently, great service is something that you do for yourself, too. It makes you feel the pride and sense of achievement that you deserve. As Norman Vincent Peale once put it: "You'll never be happy until you do something good for someone else."

Oh, and by the way, thank you for reading this chapter.

Name: _____   Date: _____

ACTIVITY #1   YOUR SERVICE QUOTIENT

What's your potential for delivering great service? Take the test below and find out. Circle the number that's closest to the way you honestly feel, then add up your total number of points at the bottom.

Most of the time I control my moods.	5 4 3 2 1	I have difficulty controlling my moods.
I'm good at remembering names and faces.	5 4 3 2 1	I have trouble remembering names or faces.
I like most people and enjoy meeting them.	5 4 3 2 1	It's hard for me to get along with other people.
I don't mind apologizing for mistakes, even if someone else made them.	5 4 3 2 1	I have trouble apologizing for some one else's mistakes.
I can be nice to people who are indifferent to me.	5 4 3 2 1	I can't be pleasant to people who aren't pleasant to me.
I enjoy being of service to others.	5 4 3 2 1	I think people should do things for themselves.
Smiling comes naturally to me.	5 4 3 2 1	I tend to be serious.
Seeing others enjoy themselves makes me happy.	5 4 3 2 1	I see no reason to please others, especially if I don't know them.
How I dress and appear to others is important to me.	5 4 3 2 1	I feel that how I dress and appear to others shouldn't be important.
I prefer communicating with others verbally.	5 4 3 2 1	I prefer communicating with others in writing.

Total number of points _____

Scoring:

46–50: You are a saint

41–45: You're excellent at service

26–40: You're very good, but could improve

11–25: You need to work at service

10: You should be an accountant or a hermit

Name: _____   Date: _____

ACTIVITY #2   LET'S TRY THIS INSTEAD

In the left-hand column is a list of "forbidden phrases." Your task: To rewrite them in as positive a way as possible.

Phrase

Your rephrasing

1. *Front desk clerk* to guest: "Sorry, but I don't know what a taxi costs from here to where you're going."

   1.

2. *Travel agent* to caller: "We're really busy right now. I wouldn't have time to look that up. You'll have to call back tomorrow morning. Okay?"

   2.

3. *Hostess at a theme restaurant* to a couple: "I'll try to get you a table, but I can't promise anything. You didn't make a reservation."

   3.

4. *Facilities manager at a Las Vegas casino* to an architect in charge of remodeling the facility: "I'm not sure why they don't want to have any windows in the casino."

   4.

5. *Museum employee* to a visitor: "You should have called in advance to find out our hours. We're closing in 15 minutes."

   5.

6. *Amtrak reservationist* to a caller: "It's company policy that we can't give you reserved seating in Coach Class."

   6.

7. *Cruise ship security officer* to travel agent who'd like to inspect the vessel while it's in port: "There's nothing I can do about getting you onboard the ship. You should have called your sales rep, and even then . . ."

   7.

8. *Tour reservationist* to caller who is wheelchair-bound: "I'll try to see if we can get you on the tour. In the meantime, I want you to call this number. It's a company that specializes in handicapped people.

   8.

6

Marketing Travel

OBJECTIVES

After reading this chapter, you'll be able to:

- Identify and explain key marketing concepts

- Apply the six major steps of the marketing cycle

- Design a marketing plan

- Interpret benchmarking, direct mail and e-mail, macro/microenvironments, push/pull strategies, relationship marketing, and Total Quality Management

Is marketing in any way relevant to you? Isn't it just a mass of theories that high-level executives translate, hopefully, into more meaningful actions?

Not really. Marketing is a far more pervasive endeavor than you might think. It touches virtually every part of your life, probably dozens of times or more each day. And if you sell to or serve the traveling public, you must fully understand how your company's marketing efforts affect what you do. The reason: Sales and service are integral components of the broader phenomenon that is marketing.

First, let's do something similar to what we did in Chapter 5. This time, without looking back, write a definition of marketing that comes as close as possible to the one you studied in Chapter 1:

Now go back to Chapter 1 and find our "official" definition. How close were you? Hopefully your definition makes you realize that marketing precedes, enfolds, and follows almost everything you might do in your work. Some examples:

- A cruise ship's food and beverage manager must interpret what the company's research has uncovered and translate that into meaningful strategies to reinforce—or change—what his personnel do and what products they should offer
- A tour manager must thoroughly familiarize herself with what the company brochure promised to her passengers
- A travel agent must respond to the image that each brand has communicated to his clients
- A DMO employee must understand how the public sees the destination he represents and predict what questions visitors typically ask (and how to answer them)
- A tour sales rep must be familiar with other tour companies. Only in this way can she position her product favorably against the competition

SOME GENERAL CONCEPTS

You may not have realized it, but you've been learning about marketing from the moment you began reading this book. Commodities, wholesaling, discretionary money, buyer motivations, tangibles, perishables, customer surveys, focus groups—all these and more are rooted in marketing. Moreover, sales and service strategies interact with and should be driven by a company's marketing vision. (Technically, they are *a part* of marketing.)

You'll be learning more about marketing in the next chapter, too. But before going any further, let's look at three general concepts that you must first know.

1. Marketing Is Both a Science and an Art

Marketing is often labeled a science, but it doesn't quite qualify. If it did, it would absolutely predict every phenomenon it encountered. Movie studio marketing experts would forecast exactly how many people would go to see a specific film, car manufacturers would know precisely which colors would attract a maximum number of buyers and TV network executives would predict which scheduling slot would draw the best ratings for a certain program.

But that doesn't happen. It's just not that simple. Since the foundation of marketing is human behavior, unpredictability will always affect results. Marketing is more like psychology or sociology than like physics, chemistry, or math. A chemist can say, "If I mix A with B, I'll get C." But a marketing expert cannot declare, with total assurance, that a specific ad campaign will lead to an exact percentage increase in sales. As with any "soft" science, marketing involves interpretation and a lot of educated guesswork about factors that are fuzzy and in constant flux.

2. Marketing Has Become Increasingly Proactive

Many companies in the past—and even a few today—simply waited to see which customers came to them and adjusted accordingly. The approach was largely a passive one. **Proactive marketing,** on the other hand, **implies that a company first decides which buyers it wants and *then* takes steps to reach them.** The business chooses where it wants to go and maps out the route to get there.

A classic example is MTV. In the late 1970s, the creators of the cable channel decided it wanted to target (that's a word you hear a lot in marketing) the 13-to-19-year-old market. But what would it offer them for viewing? Dramas featuring people of the target group's age? Interviews with young performers? Who knew? (By the way, back then, music videos were a rarity.) So MTV meticulously studied its teen market. When it went on the air, it knew rather specifically who would come to it and what they wanted. (It turned out to be music videos, lots of them.)

MTV has continued to reinvent itself as each new group of teens, with distinct preferences, has come along. Its programming has changed accordingly.

A similar example is Contiki Tours. Weren't tours just for old people? Contiki broke past that stereotype and discovered that young people liked to be with others like themselves while vacationing. It launched a tour product tailored specifically to 18- to 35-year-olds. It, too, understood its market and succeeded.

Can you think of other companies—travel or otherwise—that seem especially adept at targeting their market? The market can be broad or narrow. List two examples here:

Company   *Markets to*

1.

2.

If you chose a company with a narrowly defined market, you've identi-fied a *segment* or *niche*. More about that in Chapter 7.

Let's get back to a basic question: What is a **market? It's all the poten-tial and actual buyers of a product or service.** And what's a **target mar-ket? It's a group of buyers who share common characteristics and/or needs that a company decides to serve.**

3.   Marketing Has Relied Increasingly on Databases

A **database is an organized collection of information—usually comput-erized—about a company's customers.** It helps a company:

- Facilitate communication with customers
- Pinpoint customer buying patterns
- Identify prime customers and make special offers to them
- Provide an additional revenue source (businesses sometimes sell or exchange databases, so long as they have permission from their cus-tomers to do so)
- Communicate with customers who haven't bought for awhile to re-gain their loyalty
- Efficiently target certain customers with offers that are of specific in-terest to them

Here's an example on how, say, an Atlantic City casino-hotel uses its database for marketing purposes. The hotel tracks customer information according to frequency of stay, guest surveys, charges to room accounts and, cleverly, through its "slot club" card. When guests gamble, their cards enable them to accumulate points for prizes, depending on how much they spend.

The prime purpose of the card, however, is to *enable the hotel to precisely track each guest's patterns:* Do they gamble, how much and on which

Gaming is an important source of income to certain hotels

games? At what time of the day are they in the casino? When correlated with other data, the hotel is able to customize subsequent offers, usually made through direct mail or e-mail. One person might get an offer to stay free of charge, another for $49 weekdays, still another for $79 but with a free buffet and a show. In this way, the hotel is able to maximize on and influence the behavior of those in its database.

This kind of database marketing has enabled travel providers and others to establish more intimate and tailored communications with their customers. It's at the core of something called relationship marketing, which we'll examine later in this chapter. And it very much parallels the qualifying sales techniques you learned about in earlier chapters.

THE MARKETING CYCLE

Marketing follows a well-defined path toward its goal: to sell effectively, efficiently, and profitably. Here are the six steps that usually characterize the marketing cycle:

Marketing Step #1: Research the Demand

Is there a demand for travel? Yes, a huge one. As you learned in Chapter 1, though, that demand for travel is driven by discretionary money. Since it's not an essential, like food, shelter and clothing, travel can be strongly affected by a weak economy, a perception of danger (e.g., a terrorist act) or other, similar factors.

For instance, when the economy is doing well, people travel more for both business and leisure purposes, and hotel room rates increase. When the economy weakens, people travel less and hotel rates decrease (and fewer hotels get built).

As a result, travel providers (and the specialized research companies they use) must constantly assess and reassess the demand for their current and future offerings. Has anyone ever included you in a market research study? Describe it in a few sentences here:

Your example touches upon only one of many avenues for market research. Telephone surveys, product sampling sessions, questionnaires, focus groups and on-site interviews, among others, enable companies to understand the market that they serve. Automated, computerized systems can also capture research information about you. Credit card transactions permit companies to track your buying habits. Digital cable TV systems can monitor your viewing patterns. And it's almost impossible to

YIELD MANAGEMENT

One of the most precise ways of dealing with supply and demand is called **yield management.** It's a complicated concept, one that measures operations costs, sales revenues, and profit margins so that a company can figure out how much money it's making per customer. Armed with the resulting information, a company can figure out what its supply-demand equation is at any given point, then fine-tune its prices and offerings.

The business sector that pioneered yield management was a travel industry: the airlines. As you probably know, air ticket prices now change minute by minute, responding to the precise supply and demand measurements that yield management—and computers—have made possible.

use the Internet without unintentionally revealing information about yourself.

Huge travel suppliers, like airlines and hotel chains, regularly undertake major market research campaigns. They can afford to. But many mid-size and small travel providers don't have the money to mount costly marketing studies. Here are four things they do instead:

They Tap into Research by Others   The National Tour Association (NTA), Travel Industry of America (TIA), World Tourism Organization (WTO), Institute of Certified Travel Agents (ICTA), American Society of Travel Agents (ASTA), and Cruise Lines International Association (CLIA) regularly conduct research on behalf of their members. Travel industry magazines also carry out and publish one or two major market studies yearly. Private research firms release insightful results from their surveys. (If you want more detailed or customized information, that costs extra.) Generic market research (like some of the governmental ones cited in the previous chapter) often also contain information that companies can put to shrewd use.

By the way, when a company or association conducts its own research for a specific purpose, it's called **primary research.** Generic research that others have done—collected perhaps for another purpose—is called **secondary research.**

They Swiftly Follow Up on Trends   In the late 19th century, Thomas Cook noticed that "temperance societies" (made up of people who didn't drink alcohol) were forming throughout England. Why not offer them group departures where they could meet, discuss their philosophy, and dine at restaurants that understood their aversion to wine and beer? Today, Thomas Cook, Ltd. is a multinational conglomerate (and the temperance issue is a distant memory of the company's mission).

Another example: Ed Hogan, a former pilot, observed that Hawaii had long captured the imagination of America. If only it didn't take so many hours to get there! With the introduction of reliable ocean-hopping flights,

Hogan saw his opportunity. He founded Pleasant Hawaiian Holidays. It now does hundreds of millions of dollars worth of business yearly.

A final example: In the 1960s and '70s, the steamship industry was collapsing. Few travelers wanted to spend a week sailing across the Atlantic when they could jet across in a matter of hours. Cruise lines were going out of business, ocean liners sat idle at their docks. But several lines had "repositioned" their ships in the Caribbean for a few winter months and done rather well. (Stuck in old ways of thinking, however, those very lines would return their vessels for the rest of the year to transatlantic crossings, where they sailed half empty.) Ted Arison noticed this. He realized that ships were no longer attractive for transport; but "cruising"—that seemed more promising. With the help of loans, he bought an old ocean liner, spiffed it up and placed it in the Caribbean. One of his young executives, Bob Dickinson, called it a "Fun Ship." Thus was Carnival—a *billion* dollar company—born. And Bob Dickinson has become one of the most powerful executives in the travel industry.

All three scenarios depict someone spotting a trend at the beginning of a cycle, before anyone else did. Very little research was involved, just steely courage and a perceptive hunch.

IDENTIFYING TRENDS

Here's a challenging exercise: Is there a new, obvious trend that you perceive today in the marketplace? Identify it below and, if possible, come up with one travel product or service that could address that trend:

They Experiment Through Trial and Error Tauck Tours (now called Tauck World Discovery) has always been a pioneer in escorted tours. (**Escorted tours are those in which a tour manager accompanies a group throughout their trip and coordinates their needs.**) But it had never tried taking its customers on escorted visits to Hawaii. There were two reasons: Hawaii was far away and most visitors to Hawaii did so via **independent tours packages that consist only of air, hotel, transfers to and from the airport,** like those of Pleasant Hawaiian Holidays. After all, it was easy to experience Hawaii without the help of a tour manager.

Might there be a market for *escorted* tours to Hawaii? Tauck decided to find out. It devoted a comparatively small space of its brochure to an escorted tour to Hawaii. To Tauck's surprise, the departure filled rapidly. It then expanded the program. Today, Hawaii accounts for a major portion of Tauck's business.

Trial and error sometimes reveals a demand that no one else recognizes. It's chancy, but it's usually much cheaper than market research. And in Tauck's case it paid off in a big way.

THE ESCORTED TOUR CLIENT

What distinguishes the customers for *escorted* tours? They:

- Are very outgoing and like the idea of meeting new people
- Are drawn to enrichment (tour managers and local guides ensure that passengers will learn plenty)
- Want a no-hassle experience: no driving, no foreign language signs to decipher, etc.
- View an escorted package as a great value, with few unpredicted costs

They Imitate Others   Travel suppliers are swift to pick up on and, if possible, improve on the successful ideas of others. If one airline discovers that incorporating more legroom into the cabin increases the number of customers and enhances revenue, other airlines will do the same. When Caesars Palace in Las Vegas built a highly profitable themed shopping area (the Forum Shops), at least a half-dozen other Las Vegas resorts built themed shopping sections, too. When a few cruise lines succeeded in Alaska, others followed. Now more than twenty vessels ply Alaska's waters during the summer months.

Marketing Step #2: Develop the Product

Once a company has completed its research (or followed some of the shortcuts described above), it's time to develop or fine-tune products which meet those needs that research identified. This might, in turn, launch a whole new wave of research. But this new, second-level research won't be consumer-focused. Instead, it's more product-related. Here are some examples:

- A tour company representative visits several promising hotels at an up-and-coming destination and chooses the right one for his company. He also works out the best itinerary to and from that destination.
- A vacation-oriented lodging chain wants to open a line of properties targeted to the business traveler. It sends employees to stay at a Courtyard by Marriott, a Park Hyatt and several other competing, corporate-focused hotels. The employees inventory what they like and dislike about each. The resulting observations are correlated to market research and applied to the new line of hotels.
- A theme park intends to open a water park. It contacts manufacturers across the nation who specialize in building attractions for such parks to find out what they can offer.
- A cruise line wants to bring pizzazz to its onboard shows. Would it be possible to incorporate indoor fireworks into the presentation? What kinds would be safe? The company's director of entertainment contacts three fireworks manufacturers to find out.

Refining or developing a new travel product—or any product—can be dreadfully complicated. It involves not only product research, but countless meetings, operations development, safety procedures, employee training, supervision guidelines and thousands of other details, both large and small.

But product development, done keenly and researched thoroughly, can lead to sustained success.

Marketing Step #3: Cost the Product

Certainly this step is complicated and well beyond the scope of this book. Suffice to say that you must:

- Negotiate all prices with suppliers
- Precisely identify all costs
- Project your hoped-for number of customers
- Determine your break-even point
- Correlate all this with what your market research told you about what people are willing to pay
- Set a profit margin that's reasonable, based on what your market wants and what your company wants

The "wild card" in all this: what your market research projected regarding your customers. Will they behave differently when they *really* have to pay for your travel product? Disney certainly did careful research costing when it opened its Anaheim-based Disney's California Adventure theme park in 2001. At first, projections were on target. But after a few months, the stream of visitors began to slow. Disney quickly repriced its admission policies (providing discounts for locals) and visitors increased. The per-guest profit margin decreased, but elevated attendance figures stabilized overall profitability.

THE TWO KINDS OF COSTS

A key concept to costing: distinguishing between fixed and variable costs. **A fixed cost is one that doesn't change or hardly changes, no matter what the sales levels are.** For example, the cost of a pilot's salary is the same whether thirty or three hundred passengers are onboard. **A variable cost is one that does change according to what the sales levels are.** It does cost more to feed three hundred people on a plane than thirty.

Imagine an escorted tour. Try to list as many fixed costs you can think of and as many variable ones as you can:

Fixed Costs   Variable Costs

Marketing Step #4: Promote the Product

Things rarely sell themselves. They must be promoted to the public. In marketing terms, **promotion is the process of making consumers aware of the features, benefits, and availability of your products, with the purpose of getting them to respond to your message and buy.** To do this, you need promotional tools, like television commercials, press releases to newspapers, even sponsoring a sports facility (as American Airlines does in Miami). How you blend these tools together—and in what proportions—is called your **promotional mix.**

Try a little exercise: You're opening a company that offers motorcoach tours of Los Angeles. What seven specific tools might you use to inform visitors to L.A. about your products? We'll give you the first one to get you started:

1. *A sign outside the small building where your tours depart from*
2.

3.

4.

5.

6.

7.

Notice that we never gave you a budget. You may have wanted to hire the Goodyear Blimp as a promotional tool, but could you afford it? Not likely. Were you concerned that you had *no idea* how much certain things cost? That's normal. Anyone new to a business has to find those things out. Did you think up any low-cost or no-cost ways to promote? Great. That might allow you to spend more on other promotional tools.

And that leads us to two important definitions:

- When the promotion **costs very little or nothing** (except perhaps your time), it's called **publicity.** For example, if you designed a tour of Los Angeles for insomniacs and talked "Entertainment Tonight" into doing a little story on it (and thus getting national exposure), that's publicity. It costs you nothing.
- When the promotion **costs you something** (money or bartered), it's called **advertising.** If you took out a display ad in a magazine that's placed in most hotel rooms in the city, you paid for it. You *advertised* your services.

Three elements are critical to promotion: the **message,** the **medium,** and the **design.**

The message is what you're trying to communicate to your customers and to your prospects: we're the best cruise line; we serve the needs of the physically challenged; we believe in 100 percent satisfaction. Hot-button concepts, slogans, themes—these and more help suppliers convey their key messages to consumers.

Your message also might be reinforced by brand awareness. **A brand is a company or product whose name, image and/or reputation are well known to the public.** A good brand is almost like a warranty. And it makes your buying decision easier and quicker.

Carefully calculated promotion is the key to brand awareness.

Let's prove it. Try to identify each of the following brands from their slogans:

1. Have it your way:

2. It's the real thing:

3. The Love Boat:

4. Built _____ tough:

5. You're in good hands:

6. We try harder:

7. The office superstore:

8. They melt in your mouth, not in your hands:

9. Must-see TV:

10. We'll leave the light on for you:

COLORFUL MESSAGES

Do colors have a significant impact on how a promotional message is perceived? Here's a list of colors and what they supposedly communicate. Do you agree with the experts?

- White: Purity, professionalism, cleanliness, sanctity
- Black: Mystery, authority, strength, loyalty
- Gray: Subtlety, understatement, dignity, corporateness
- Red: Excitement, love, fulfillment, passion
- Burgundy: Exotic, romance, toned-down emotion
- Yellow: Fun, esteem, confidence, sunniness, warmth
- Orange: Warmth, power, action, mature emotion
- Brown, tan: Earthiness, mature professionalism, traditional, solid
- Blue: Tenderness, caring, honesty, control, water-related
- Green: Youthfulness, leisure, health, friendship, nature-related
- Purple: Royalty, frugality, security, dignity, nonconformity
- Gold, silver: Quality, expense, luxury, prestige

Some of these slogans have been "retired," yet you probably got them right anyway. Such is the power of slogans, brands and their messages. (By the way, **the *value* to a company that a brand has to generate awareness and communicate quality is called brand equity.**) People usually buy what is most familiar to them. That's what brand equity is all about.

Equally essential to product promotion is the *medium* you utilize. **A medium is the "channel" you use to communicate your message.** It can be *display media* (e.g., posters, signs, billboards), *broadcast media* (e.g., e-mail, TV, radio) or *print media* (e.g., brochures, newspapers, magazines, direct mail).

The third factor that's critical to promotion is *design:* **Design is how you artistically present your message for maximum effect.** What key color should you use? Which typeface? What music is ideal for your radio ad? Which kind of narrator voice should you use? Peppy? Mature? Man or woman? Design requires countless little choices, yet each of these choices will have enormous implications for the effectiveness of your promotion.

MARKETING DISCONNECT

One phenomenon that plagues today's marketing is called **marketing disconnect.** It occurs when a company's marketing team does a great job of giving promotional "spin" to their message, yet fails to communicate and implement that message on a front-line level. Some examples:

- You call an airline reservations department and wait on hold for fourty minutes, listening to an overly cheery voice recording that assures you that the airline considers customers like you *so* important.
- You take a tour of Paris. The brochure promises "You'll have plenty of time to visit the Louvre." That time turns out to be fourty-five minutes for one of the world's largest museums.
- A chain of travel agencies boasts of how professional and knowledgeable its travel agents are, yet the agent you call confuses Austria with Australia.
- A hotel chain says that every one of its properties has a health facility. You stay at one where that facility consists of one treadmill and a mismatched set of dumbbells, in a poorly ventilated room, with a TV that has a snowy picture.

Some marketing disconnect happens in every business. Problems arise, however, when marketing executives work in a vacuum, conjuring catchy promotions that have no relationship to reality. A wise company ensures that the message it communicates reflects actual performance. If it doesn't, then that company should take clearly defined steps toward the intended performance that its new promotional message promises.

Marketing Step #5: Distribute and Sell the Product

Distribution is how you make your product available to consumers. In some industries—especially those that sell tangibles—this process requires complicated procedures.

Let's say yours is a candy company based in Belgium. You want to sell your gourmet candy bars in America. What must you do to distribute them? You wrap them, box them, crate them, load them onto a truck that takes them to a ship. The ship carries your crates of candy bars across the Atlantic to New York City. After paying a duty tax, the bars are loaded onto train cars that take them to different warehouses across America, where they're unloaded and stored. As needed, they're loaded onto trucks that transport them to stores, where they're unloaded, priced, and placed on shelves. The customer picks up a bar and puts it into his shopping basket. Eventually he takes it to the checkout stand, where the bar is scanned and the customer pays. The bar is placed in a bag with the shopper's other purchases. Only then has the distribution process ended.

Distributing an intangible like travel is so much easier. A supplier creates a travel product and sells it directly to the public and/or indirectly through an intermediary, like a travel agency or tour operator. There's no tangible thing to move. It's that simple.

Also, it's critical to distribution that you make your product easy to buy. Customers want their buying experience to be simple. If you have inflexible purchase procedures, provide limited buying options, or put too many barriers in the way, the buyer will simply go somewhere else.

Marketing Step #6: Follow Up

Follow-up is essential to selling, to service and, yes, to marketing. As you've learned, it ensures customer satisfaction, builds loyalty, and often sets the stage for the next sale.

Unfortunately, it's often the forgotten step of marketing. It takes time, money, and effort. It sometimes brings to light problems you wished you hadn't heard (but that you should). Yet over and again, follow-up proves its worth.

A CLIA study surveyed people who had bought their second cruise from a different travel agency than they did the first one. Why did they shift allegiance? Twenty-six percent said because of poor service. Twenty-five percent said: "Because the travel agent never called me back to see how things went." All other reasons trailed these two.

MARKETING PLANS

Have you ever seen the 1996 movie *Jerry Maguire*? Its plot revolves almost entirely around the efforts of its central character (played by Tom Cruise) to fashion a marketing plan. How do you define it? **A marketing plan is a written description of a company's objectives and how these objectives will be achieved.**

Here are the steps—in a highly simplified form—that generally constitute a marketing plan. To clarify each step, let's apply it to a hypothetical ecotour company.

1. The Executive Summary

This section presents a brief overview of the entire marketing plan. It sets the stage for what's to come and enables those with limited time to familiarize themselves with the plan's key points.

2. The Mission Statement

This spells out the company's philosophy and what it intends to accomplish. Whenever possible, these goals—especially the financial ones—are stated in measurable terms.

For our ecotour company, the mission might be to provide high-quality, environmentally sensitive expeditions to destinations that appeal to ecologically minded travelers. The measurable goal would be to increase the number of customers by 25 percent yearly for five years, with an average net yearly profit margin of 18 percent.

3. The Market Situation

This section examines research, both by the company and from other sources, on the current and future market conditions. It also analyzes how attractive that market is.

Our ecotour company would assert that the market for ecological travel is growing rapidly and that the supply of eco-themed travel products has yet to catch up with demand. Pursuing this market opportunity promises a high degree of success.

4. The SWOT Analysis

A SWOT analysis is a remarkable little tool to further define the environment a company works in. This acronym stands for:

- **S**trengths: What the company is especially good at
- **W**eaknesses: What the company doesn't do especially well
- **O**pportunities: What factors a company might capitalize on
- **T**hreats: What might interfere with the company's success

Our hypothetical ecotour company could list as its *strengths*: an expert managerial staff, creative itineraries, solid supplier relationships, a loyal customer base, and a reputation for keen environmental awareness.

Weaknesses might be an inexperienced guide staff, accommodations that are somewhat inconsistent, and a lackluster Web site.

Opportunities might include more alliances with ecologically themed stores (e.g., the Nature Company), as well as increased business through travel agencies. (As with many specialized suppliers, the vast majority of eco-business comes directly from customers, with no intermediaries.)

Among the possible *threats*: The fact that several major tour operators plan to introduce specialized lines of nature-themed travel products. Several institutions (e.g., National Geographic) are studying the possibility of operating their own group departures. And about a half-dozen eco-specialized companies have firmly established themselves in the marketplace.

5. Customer Analysis

This portion of the marketing plan explores the demographic and psychographic makeup of current customers and projects how these might change in the future. (We'll discuss demographics and psychographics in Chapter 7.)

Our ecotour operator's research indicates that its typical client is, among other things, between 50 and 65 years old, married, college educated, belongs to several associations, leads an active, fit lifestyle, has an annual household income of $70,000 to $100,000, and is strongly concerned about the environment.

6. The Marketing Mix

Earlier in this chapter you learned about the promotional mix: how a company blends its promotional tools. A promotional mix is just one part of a broader feature of a marketing plan, the **marketing mix.**

Before getting to the marketing mix, let's backtrack for a moment. Now that you know a little about our imaginary ecotour operator, what four promotional tools might you concentrate on to get the company's message across? Remember: This is still a smallish company with limited dollars for promotion.

Example: Run an ad in an eco-newsletter, *The Environmental Traveler*

1.

2.

3.

4.

So here you have described your promotional mix. This, in turn, becomes one element out of five P's that constitute the *marketing mix:*

- **Product:** The kinds of things you sell
- **Price:** What you charge for your products
- **Promotion:** How you get the word out
- **Place:** Where you sell it
- **Position:** How you develop a clear, unique, attractive, and well-defined image among consumers

All these come together to create a company's marketing approach.

PRICING

Travel products don't have *a* price. They usually have many prices. Here's a rundown:

- **"Official" prices.** This is what something costs "in theory." It's sort of like the "suggested retail prices" found in other businesses. In travel, these most often appear in cruise or tour brochures, as the "rack rate" of a hotel room, or full fare on a flight. Except in times of extremely high demand (e.g., lodging in a city hosting the Super Bowl—when prices may even rise above the "official" price) or at the last minute (e.g., full price for a flight), consumers rarely pay this rate.
- **Discounted prices.** These occur often and for many reasons: for bookings made well in advance; for members of a certain society or organization; because product is not selling well (e.g., a cruise ship is sailing in a few weeks at only 60 percent capacity); because of the buyer's age (such as child or senior fares); during times of low demand (e.g., a weekend for an airport hotel, a cruise the week after Christmas); attendance at a convention, etc. A **promotional rate** is a discounted price used to stimulate sales.
- **Negotiated corporate prices.** Companies or government entities that purchase in volume from a travel provider usually negotiate a special, lower rate for its employees.
- **Negotiated business-to-business prices.** Travel companies buy from other travel companies at reduced rates. For example, a tour company can buy tickets from an airline at a discount and fold them into its package price. Travel agency chains also contract with travel providers for special deals, which they can pass on to customers (sometimes at a markup).
- **Group prices.** Most travel providers offer lower prices to those who put together a special group departure (e.g., a club, a travel agency, or even a family).
- **Internet-only rates.** Many companies offer rates that are only available on their Web sites. The reason: because it involves almost no personnel time, the cost to execute the transaction is much, much lower than with a reservationist.
- **Controlled price offers.** These are discounted rates that travel suppliers post on the Internet (often at an auction site) or send out via mail, e-mail, or fax, either to agents or directly to consumers. The idea is to reach their loyal or targeted customers, not the general public.
- **Industry prices.** Most suppliers offer discounts to travel professionals, especially if they are productive (e.g., a cruise discount rate to a travel agent who sells a lot of their product). Often the best discounts occur at periods of shoulder (medium) or low demand. (Sometimes industry rates are called familiarization rates, or fam rates.)

Positioning   Many decades ago, some enterprising salespeople wanted a way to set apart a brand of cookies. They thought up the idea of making the cookies in animal shapes and then came up with the brilliant notion of packaging them in a box that resembled a circus cage railroad car. Thus were born animal crackers, perhaps the most memorable biscuits ever known. Now *that's* positioning.

Of the five P's, position has become even more critical today than it was in animal cracker times. The reason: So many products clutter the marketplace today that it's hard to tell one from the other. Why choose one over another if they're all alike?

To meet this challenge, marketers try to identify and promote that distinctive something that will give them a competitive advantage. To do this, they follow two approaches:

- **True positioning** means that the company offers a product that's genuinely different from typical products in its category. Our ecotour operator, for example, would be well positioned, since it's not like the typical mass-market tour. (It would, however, have to find ways to set itself apart from other ecotour companies.)
- **Pseudo positioning** avows that the product is very similar to its competitors, but differentiates itself through superficial tactics. For example, Tide detergent uses an orange box and bullseye-like logo to distinguish itself from other detergents. Coca-Cola, from almost the very beginning, has relied on an unusually shaped bottle to position itself among colas. Yahoo! positions itself from competitors through its outrageous name.

    As author Harry Beckwith points out, the more similar the products, the more important the differences—even trivial ones—are. If customers can't identify a company's position, then that company is in trouble.

Closely allied to positioning is the concept of theming. **Theming is the process of applying a distinctive, pervasive, and entertaining motif to a travel-related experience.** Can you think of any well-known themed experiences in the following categories? We've given one example for each. In the last column, come up with an additional example for each category:

Experience	*Our example/theme*	*Your example/theme*
Dining	The House of Blues (music theme)	
Theme park	Disneyland's various areas: Tomorrowland (sci-fi theme); Frontierland (Western theme)	
Hotel	The Luxor, Las Vegas (Egyptian theme)	

THEMING, POSITIONING, AND LAS VEGAS

A classic example of pseudo positioning: the casino-hotels of Las Vegas. In reality, most are virtually identical: thousands of rooms, hundreds of slot machines, big buffets, lots of shops, entertainment venues and, for many, a Y-shaped hotel structure. So how can prospects tell one hotel from the other? Through superficial attributes that really have nothing to do with the core lodging product itself.

So what positions some major Las Vegas resorts?

- *The Mirage:* A volcano in front and white tigers within (inside of an enclosure, of course)
- *The Rio:* An all-suite hotel (even though most rooms aren't traditional suites)
- *The Venetian:* Looks like Venice, complete with gondolas and canals
- *New York-New York:* Built to resemble the New York skyline
- *Treasure Island:* A pirate-naval battle out front four times daily
- *Paris Las Vegas:* The "City of Lights" in another city of lights

In this manner, each casino resort can claim a different, superficial personality that distinguishes it in the marketplace.

The Luxor is a prime example of themed lodging. (*Photo by Marc Mancini*)

7. Strategies and Actions

A good marketing plan leads to a clearly justified series of strategies and subsequent actions for the company to undertake. These actions may address all sorts of issues that the marketing plan brought up: personnel, advertising media, targeting new customers, addressing certain opportunities, perhaps overcoming a weakness.

To define its action list, a company or organization often seeks answers to the following questions:

- **What** action will be taken?
- **Who** will be responsible for each action?
- **When** will it be done?
- **Where** will the actions take place?
- **How much** will it cost?
- **How long** will it take?

Did you notice something? The very same questions a salesperson asks when determining the needs of a client also apply to marketing.

A marketing plan is a company's roadmap to success. The roadmap we've just given you lists only the major "roads." If you wish to learn about marketing plans in depth, you should consider the many fine publications and computer programs that are available and that can teach you, in great detail, how to forge an effective and productive marketing plan.

MARKETING MISCELLANY

Up to this point, you've learned quite a bit in this chapter's "crash course" on marketing. Here are a few additional concepts, with thumbnail descriptions, that are integral to today's business environment:

Business Plans

After reading the previous section, you should have a good sense of what a marketing plan is all about. But what's a *business* plan? **A business plan is an extended, comprehensive document that companies develop to guide them financially and to help them get bank loans.** It includes the marketing plan, plus such elements as employee resources, financial statements, tax returns, assets (e.g., equipment), income and cash flow projections, expenses and budget controls.

Benchmarking

Want to find out how you're doing against the competition? Benchmarking helps you achieve that. **Benchmarking occurs when a company analyzes what competitors and leading companies in other industries are doing, with the purpose of setting new standards and adopting new strategies for success.**

For example, Orlando's visitors bureau might analyze how Hawaii markets itself. It would discover that Hawaii has shifted much of its promotion to the Internet, targeted special-interest groups and developed a print-based training program for travel agents—all with great success. These "best practices" become the foundation of the Orlando visitors bureau's new approach.

Direct Mail and E-Mail

Direct mail refers to the letters, brochures, postcards, flyers or other, similar items that a company sends through the mail directly to consumers or businesses. Though the idea is simple, doing it effectively and right is a much different matter. Indeed, an entire science has arisen around direct mail marketing. Some of its discoveries:

- The PS is the second thing most people read in a letter (even before reading the body of the letter)
- The average person spends seven seconds deciding whether or not to open an envelope
- Red or blue envelopes are more likely to be opened than white ones
- An envelope with a real stamp attracts prospects more than one with metered postage. So do envelopes that are hand-addressed
- Mail that arrives at a home on Friday or Saturday is more likely to be read than mail arriving on other days of the week

In some cases, companies have replaced direct mail pieces with e-mail. The reason: It's much less expensive and time-consuming. There's nothing to print and no postage is required. It's also easy to forward; e-mail is an ideal vehicle for word-of-mouth promotions. One drawback, however, is that not all households have access to the Internet.

What characterizes effective e-mail?

- **E-mail must be timely.** It's most effective when it brings news about something very current, like an upcoming one-day airfare sale.

- **E-mail must be well timed.** E-mail to homes works best on Friday afternoons; to businesses it's first thing in the morning, Tuesday through Friday.
- **E-mail must be targeted.** The offer or information should be sent only to those most likely to respond.
- **E-mail should be customized.** As with direct mail, personalizing the message makes it more effective.
- **E-mail must be concise.** Readers want to spend only a brief time understanding what your message is about.
- **Get the customer's permission.** "Spam" (unsolicited e-mail) often provokes resentment. Ask the reader first for permission before sending e-correspondence.
- **Include a link.** A hyperlink to your Web site should facilitate the reader's response.
- **Track, measure, and react to e-mail response.** Communication works only if it results in a quick response and yields valuable marketing data.

Macroenvironments and Microenvironments

These commonly used marketing terms are less complicated than they sound. **A macroenvironment describes the major, outside forces in a society that affect a business.** Some examples:

- An economic boom drives more people to book travel through travel agencies
- A terrorist threat curtails tourism to a particular destination
- A high birthrate increases family travel to a theme park for several years
- An especially harsh winter in the northern United States and Canada leads to increased visitors from those places to the sunny, warm Caribbean

There's not much a business can do to affect macro forces, but it *certainly must respond to them.* For instance, a cruise line might plan to expand its onboard children's activities in response to a high birthrate.

A microenvironment describes the forces internal to or close to a company that affect its business. Some examples:

- Internal: Staff, management, accounting
- Close: Suppliers, customers, competitors

In some cases (especially with internal forces), a company can indeed control its micro situation. In theory, it should be able to influence close forces, too, though such control takes coordinated and farsighted efforts.

Push vs. Pull Strategy

When a company promotes its products primarily to intermediaries, who then promote it to consumers, this is called a **push strategy.** For example, a tour operator may choose to do little or no advertising to the public, instead building relationships with travel agencies, which will promote and

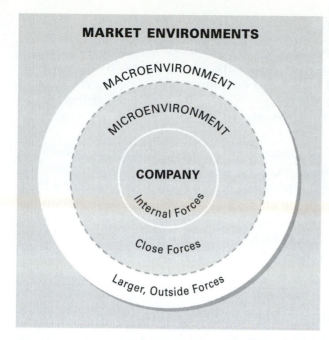

sell its tours for it. The demand for the product or service starts primarily at the intermediary level. It will be "pushed" toward customers.

In a **pull strategy,** a company spends most of its advertising funds on consumer promotions to build up demand. The idea: Customers will become aware of and desire that company's products and go to their local travel agency (or directly to the company) to buy. The demand for the product starts primarily at the consumer level. It will "pull" customers to the company's products.

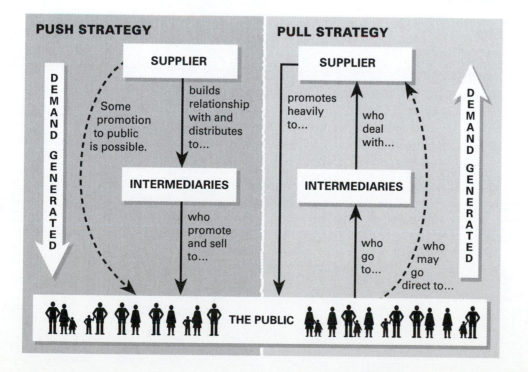

Relationship Marketing

The often-used phrase, **relationship marketing,** describes **a strategy where a company is dedicated to creating, maintaining, nurturing and enhancing the business it does with customers.** The reason: A satisfied, loyal, long-term customer is a huge business asset. Once difficult and time-consuming, relationship marketing has become far easier to achieve through databases.

One type of relationship marketing we briefly examined earlier is called a **loyalty program** (also known as a *patronage* or *frequent-buyer program*). A classic example: Frequent-flyer programs give a forceful reason for a traveler to limit flights to one airline and its partners. Beyond this, frequent-flyer programs also result in sending customers regular communications, special offers and the like, all of which reinforce the loyalty.

Just remember: You don't really sell travel products. You sell a relationship.

Total Quality Management (TQM)

Pioneered by economist W. Edwards Demming and made famous by firms in postwar Japan, **Total Quality Management (TQM)** argues that a company must constantly improve its processes, products, and services to stay competitive. TQM is a science unto itself, with very specific steps (e.g., flowcharting and "quality teams"). TQM became famous in the travel industry through its implementation at the highly successful Ritz-Carlton hotel chain.

So there it is: marketing in a nutshell. Know that marketing practices are in constant evolution. The ideas of today may grow overused, stale and, eventually, ineffective. Other marketing strategies will almost surely become popular and affect the way companies connect with their customers.

Name: _____   Date: _____

ACTIVITY #1   POSITIONING THE CRUISE LINES

Below are the Web site addresses of five cruise lines. Based on the information they give, try to fig-ure out how each line has positioned itself as unique in the marketplace. We've given you one ex-ample to start with.

Cruise Line   **Position**

1. Seabourn Cruise Line: *Provider of super-luxury experiences on small ships,*
   www.seabourn.com   *with a strong focus on destinations*

2. Peter Deilmann Cruises:
   www.deilmann-cruises.com

3. Windstar Cruises:
   www.windstarcruises.com

4. Cruise West:
   www.cruisewest.com

5. Norwegian Coastal Voyage:
   www.coastalvoyage.com

Name: _____   Date: _____

ACTIVITY #2   SORTING THE MAIL

For one week, carefully track all the promotional mail you receive. Analyze your own behavior: Which pieces do you pay attention to, which ones do you ignore and *why*? Describe four below. We've given you an example.

Describe the piece of mail	**Describe your behavior and why**
Example: Postcard for semi-annual clothing sale. You must bring in the postcard for an extra 10 percent off. Name and address was handwritten, not typed.	*I read it, largely because the message was so simple. Don't think I'll need new clothes, but I kept it just in case.*

1.

2.

3.

4.

7

Special Topics

OBJECTIVES

After reading this chapter, you'll be able to:

- Sell effectively through the Internet

- Apply twelve tactics to telephone sales and service

- Target niche markets and clients

- Meet corporate travelers' needs

- Sell to groups and incentives

- Use seven strategies to write effectively

- Adjust to challenging times

Not everything in travel sales, service, and marketing fits into neat little categories. Certain topics are so contemporary, important, or unique that they deserve a separate section. So here are seven advanced topics that merit your special attention and that will refine your ability to connect with your customers.

SELLING ON THE INTERNET

Have you ever booked any of the following on the Internet? Check all that apply:

❏ Air ticket
❏ Car rental
❏ Hotel
❏ Theme park admission
❏ All-inclusive resort

❏ Cruise
❏ Independent fly-drive tour
❏ Escorted tour
❏ Rail journey
❏ Other: _____

If you're like most people, the greatest likelihood is that you've booked air tickets, hotels and/or car rentals on the Internet. This goes back to what you learned in Chapter 1: Consumers feel comfortable about purchasing commodities (products and services that are simple, similar and distinguished almost only by price) without consultative assistance. The Internet is supremely adept at facilitating such transactional sales. That's why air tickets, car rentals, and hotel lodging account for the vast majority of Internet sales. (That's also why you might buy milk at a 7-Eleven or a garden chair at Target. Who needs help for such things?)

The public, however, is still uncomfortable about buying complex, unfamiliar, or pricey travel experiences on the Internet. They need advice, consultation, expert opinions, problem-solving, and the personal touch. To fulfill those desires, they need some*one*, not some*thing*. That's why cruises, tours, and FITs continue to be sold in person or over the phone, usually by travel agents. Just about the only consumers who feel very comfortable buying experiential travel products on the Internet are those who:

- *Always* plan all of their travel (do-it-yourselfers)
- Understand the product in question very well (e.g., frequent cruisers)
- Are responding to an Internet-only sale price
- Feel so comfortable with the Internet that they buy virtually everything on-line

Internet Patterns

Other patterns have clearly emerged in Internet sales. Among them:

- **Consumers use the Internet for travel research more than for travel buying.** Web sites are a terrific source of just about anything you need to know about travel. However, the public is suspicious about whether Internet information is accurate, timely, and unbiased. (Privacy and security are issues, too.) Sure, Acme Cruise Lines makes its staterooms look great, its service impeccable, and its cuisine divine. But is that reality? Often, people are more likely to trust a travel agent or even a phone reservationist than a supplier's slick Web pages.
- **Price is a major consideration for Web buyers,** especially when commodities are involved. In essence, Web buyers are choosing self-service over a personalized buying situation that *perhaps* will be more costly. (Tests have proved, over and over, that a travel agent is generally more adept at finding the best deal than someone who does it himself.)

One other factor: Many travel suppliers have chosen a direct-to-the-public-via-the-Internet strategy. Not only do they wish consumers to bypass travel agents (to whom they must pay a commission) but also would like the public to bypass the company's *own phone sales representatives* (to whom the company must pay a salary). To achieve this, they offer Internet-only prices and special promotional sales that a customer cannot obtain from an agent or phone reservationist. This is especially common in the airline and car rental industries.

THE INTERNET PROFIT EQUATION

Why do some suppliers try to move sales onto the Internet, while others don't? It all comes down to distribution costs. Auto rental companies have found that, to execute a booking, a travel agent sale may cost them $15, a company reservationist transaction $8 and an Internet transaction 10 to 20 cents.

On the other hand, cruise lines discovered that consumers rarely booked staterooms on-line. People did their research, then telephoned the cruise line's own reservationists. The first call typically lasted ten to fifteen minutes and was followed by five more calls. The conclusion: "Let travel agents handle most of our sales. That's what the public wants, and it will be less expensive for us in the long run."

- **The Internet's virtual shopping experience is highly appealing.** That you can interact with product information without sales pressure is a real plus to many shoppers. You can even access real-time views from cruise ships or watch a flight as it crosses a world map. Such features outstrip anything a brochure can achieve.
- **Convenience is a major benefit to Internet buying.** The ability to book from your home or office, 24/7, without waiting on hold or for a call back, appeals mightily to those who buy on the Internet.
- **The Internet is especially popular with do-it-yourselfers.** Many vacationers prefer putting together their own trips—and did so long before the Internet, usually by using toll-free phone numbers. That's why most suppliers have concluded that many of those who purchase travel via the Web have "migrated" from those suppliers' toll-free phone reservation systems, rather than from travel agents.

What Works Best for Web-Based Sales and Marketing?

It's astonishing how guidelines for good Web selling and marketing have emerged so swiftly. Here are twelve "rules" of Web site design that have proved effective.

1. **Build a relationship.** Yes, the relationship approach to marketing applies to Internet use, too. A customer must enjoy, trust and repeatedly return to a Web site for it to be successful.
2. **Keep it simple.** Use bullet points, empty "white space" and easy-to-read fonts to keep the look clean and uncluttered. Avoid color combinations that are hard to read (e.g., yellow over a white background).

Don't clutter the page with dense prose or overcomplicated words. Remember: People don't read a Web page as a linear, printed document—their gaze tends to fall on whatever is interesting, no matter where it is on the screen.

3. **Make it entertaining.** Travel is fun. So travel Web sites should entertain the prospect with cleverness, colors, images, animation, sound effects, and other lively elements. Remember, though: Too many "bells and whistles" slow page downloading.

4. **Make it user-friendly.** A Web site should load easily and fast. The site should also be simple to navigate. It must make it effortless for users to return to the home page after they've delved deeper into the site. It should not require a visitor to provide a lot of personal information before allowing access to the site.

5. **Customize to your customers.** The look, feel, and text of a Web site must match what you sell and to whom you're selling it. A resort targeted to young people? Use vibrant colors, dynamic images, and hot buttons specific to the niche. Selling to older, affluent clients? Take a more sedate, refined approach.

THE INTERNET VS. TRAVEL AGENCIES

Are the Internet and travel agencies enemies? Hopefully not. This very attitude in another business (movie studios vs. television) virtually destroyed the film industry in the 1950s and '60s. As soon as the studios recognized that they could be suppliers of programming to television networks, their financial woes were largely over. That old conflict now seems absurd—the lines between entertainment sectors are totally blurred.

So, too, will those between "virtual" and "real" sellers of travel (or as many call them, "click" or "brick" companies). Already, mega-agency chains sell plenty of travel on their Web sites. Tourist bureaus refer inquiries to "agent specialists." And travel intermediaries who began as on-line companies now regularly hire agents to supplement their e-services (especially when selling cruises and tours).

6. **Encourage interactivity.** Establish a link for e-mail communication. Incorporate a game into the site. Allow the visitor to view your product through a live video link (e.g., a "pool cam" at a resort). Create self-assessment activities that help users understand their buying styles and that recommend the right products for each of those customers.

7. **Provide several ways for your customer to buy.** Integrate on-line booking capability into the site, but give the visitor alternative channels (phone, fax, e-mail and, if appropriate, in-person) to ask questions or to make that booking.

8. **Keep it error-free.** Accurate grammar and spelling reflect your professionalism. So proofread those Web pages carefully.

9. **Keep the information rich.** Though it should be tightly presented, information is one of the key assets of a Web site. Links to other sites can help you expand your content—just make sure that users can easily find their way back to your site. Provide a Frequently Asked Questions (FAQ) page. FAQs seem especially conducive to Web site communication.

10. **Review and update.** One of the Internet's strengths—as opposed to, say, a brochure—is that you can update information at a moment's notice. A Web site that seems poorly maintained and stale will turn off a visitor. Every few weeks you should review your entire site to determine what might need to be changed. You should also make new offers regularly—it will give clients a reason to revisit your site.

11. **Help consumers find you.** Appealing to search engines has become a science unto itself. Choose your site title very carefully. Keep your keywords simple. Give each page on your site different and precise keywords, each based on the theme of that page. Put your keyword text before any graphics. Remember: Internet strategies change quickly. Keep up on the latest approaches.

12. **Promote your Web address everywhere.** Ads, newsletters, brochures, business cards, Yellow Pages—all your promotional avenues should herald your Web site.

One final thing about the Internet: Travel has become one of the top products sold on-line. The Internet's influence and importance to the future of the travel industry—despite its limitations—will continue to grow at a prodigious rate.

PHONE SALES

For decades now, phone sales have dominated the travel distribution system. Even with the emergence of the Internet, the telephone has continued to be a preeminent buying and service tool. Why? Write three reasons you think people continue to use the telephone so much:

1.

2.

3.

However, the phone does indeed have its limitations:

- **The buyer and seller can't see each other.** Imagine you had to talk to someone with your hands tied and blindfolded. In a way, that's what happens on the phone. Since over 50 percent of communication is visual, telephones drain the sales process of its subtlety. Posture, gestures, facial expressions—all of these are lost.
- **Phone communications can be frustratingly inefficient.** You're put on hold, then disconnected. Or you wait forever. Or you have to push buttons over and again to navigate through automated choices. Or you must listen to insipid music or incessant recorded sales pitches.
- **Phone communications invite distractions.** Ever get annoyed when you hear someone doing things on the other end of the line? The phone discourages attention. The buyer and seller simply aren't "there" as they would be in a face-to-face transaction.

Exacerbating this is the fact that, according to a Verizon study, 90 percent of businesspeople have never received phone skills training.

Whether you're in front-line-to-the-public, business-to-business or within-business sales, you must perfect your telephone skills. Here are twelve telephone tactics that can help you achieve that:

1. **Use the ideal greeting.** As you learned in Chapter 2, researchers know what the perfect greeting is. It's: "Good morning (or afternoon), (your company's name or your division in that company), this is (your name). How may I help you?"

   Why does this work? To review and expand on what you've already read:
   - "Good morning" is friendlier and more emotionally positive than "hello."
   - Giving your company's name reassures callers that they dialed the right number. It also reinforces the company's name in the caller's mind.
   - Your name personalizes the call and increases the likelihood that buyers will give you their names.
   - "How may I help you," an open-ended question, positions you as caring, suggests possibilities, and sets the stage for a wide-reaching, consultative type of sale.

2. **Sprinkle *you* and *me* throughout the conversation.** Words like these link buyer and seller. They're one more way to personalize the somewhat detached nature of a telephone call.

3. **Once you know it, use the client's name.** This, too, personalizes a call. Don't overdo it, though. The best times to use the customer's name: early in the conversation; when you make your recommendation; near the agreement stage; and at the very end of the sale.

4. **Picture the caller in your mind.** It's important for you to react to a person, not a voice. If you visualize the customer—it doesn't matter whether you get it right—then it'll be easier to relate to your buyer.

5. **Be energetic.** Robbed of your visual expressions, it's hard to convey excitement over the phone. So you must be *extra* energetic. Remember: The buyer is excited about the trip. Reinforce that excitement.

6. **Speak with a smile.** Isn't it odd? Callers can "hear" a smile. (That's why voice-over actors try to smile when narrating commercials.) A second benefit: Psychologists have actually proven that the act of smiling releases pleasure-provoking endorphins into our bloodstreams. Smiling actually makes you feel better.

7. **Be noisy.** Have you been in a situation where you weren't sure that the listener was still on the other end of the line because you weren't hearing any sounds? "Uh huh," "yes," "okay" reassure the caller that you're right there with them.

8. **Take notes.** Note-taking forces you to focus on what the caller is saying.

9. **Mirror the caller's verbal pace.** The speed at which people talk reflects how they value time. You must mimic their pace. It'll keep you in harmony with the buyer.

10. **Cultivate a professional appearance.** This seems to make no sense. The caller can't see you. Yet, somehow, salespeople project their grooming attitudes over the phone. You should dress, move, groom and pose in almost the same way as you would if the client were right there with you.

11. **Use comfortable telephone equipment.** Headsets are much more user-friendly than hand-held receivers. And avoid talking on a speakerphone. It alienates most callers. That's the last thing you want to do with a customer.

12. **If appropriate and feasible, give the caller a reason to come to see you.** This is especially relevant to travel agents, who have a much better chance of forging an agreement with a client if that client visits the agency in person. One way to do it: Tell them about a video you could loan to them that would help them plan their trip. This also applies to business-to-business selling. If you're offering something to the representative of a company you deal with, you should—if logistically and financially possible—offer to visit them at an appointed time and date.

Your key consideration when dealing with telephone sales: What you say is important, but *how* you say it may be even more crucial.

NICHE MARKETING AND SALES

Think of a shopping mall you're especially familiar with. List at least five of its stores that come to mind—but don't list any department stores:

1.

2.

3.

4.

5.

Almost surely at least some—probably all—of the stores you listed specialize in very narrowly defined categories of products. For example, if you wrote Cinnabon, you've identified a highly specialized business: cinnamon rolls. If you cited Foot Locker, you know that they concentrate on athletic shoes.

This approach to marketing and sales is called **segmentation** (a term usually used by marketers), **specialty retailing** or—particularly in the travel business—**niche marketing.** Niche marketing is the direct opposite of **mass marketing,** which seeks to attract the greatest number of possible buyers. Once it was the *only* way things were sold. (Henry Ford once quipped that he'd be happy to provide his customers with a Model-T in any color, so long as it was black.) Mass marketing does survive, to some extent, in such businesses as department stores, major TV networks (NBC, ABC, and CBS) and newspaper publishing.

Let's do another exercise. Below is a list of industries. For each business, try to come up with at least one company that markets to a *specialized* segment of its industry. (The more specialized, the better.) Try, also, to identify one kind of person it targets. Do not repeat any from the previous exercise.

Industry	Company	Product/service	Targets . . .
1. Example: Footwear	*Foot Locker*	*Athletic shoes*	*Fitness/active types*
2. Example: Retail stores	*Toys "R" Us*	*Toys*	*Children (and their parents)*

3. Cable TV

4. Apparel

5. Magazine
   publishing

6. Restaurants

7. Radio
   broadcasting

8. Beverages

9. Furniture

10. Cruise industry

Review the target customers you listed in the right-hand column. Almost surely you can classify each according to . . .

1. **Lifestyle:** A way of living that reflects a person's likes, attitudes, and values. It often embodies what a person does with his or her leisure time.
2. **Lifestage:** The period of a person's life, especially in the way age determines that person's likes, attitudes and values.

Using Examples 1 and 2 of the previous exercise, Foot Locker addresses the needs of someone with an *active lifestyle*. (It also meets the needs of those who do a lot of walking, standing, etc.) Toys R Us targets the needs of those at a *childhood lifestage* (and parents, who are in a lifestage, too: parenthood).

Of course, the two can and do overlap. Fitness-seekers are more common at certain lifestages and children do have a certain lifestyle. (Play and learning are especially important to them.)

Another approach that illuminates niche sales and marketing is to divide it into *demographics* (easily measurable criteria, such as age, gender, income level, marital status, etc.) and *psychographics* (harder-to-measure criteria, such as beliefs, values, opinions, desires, and the like). Lifestages are often driven by demographics (specifically, age), while lifestyles have more to do with psychographics.

Demographics and psychographics also often intersect. A travel company might target people who enjoy tours and like to golf, are over 50 years old, wealthy, and married. What makes such segmentation possible today are computer databases, which you learned about in Chapter 6.

Marketers can now easily carve down a vast mailing list into an extremely targeted one, one that helps them reach the very narrowly defined groups that their product will most appeal to. Without computers, this would have required a daunting amount of time to accomplish. Today, it's quite achievable.

WHAT DETERMINES A BUYER'S VALUES?

One of the great debates among economists is this: *What most determines the way a person thinks and buys?* Traditional scholars argue that our beliefs change according to our age. An oft-quoted example: Young people tend to be liberal-thinking because they have few assets to protect, no long-standing life patterns, and are naturally attracted to change. As they grow older, though, they become more conservative, since change would threaten their assets and disrupt their well-ordered lives. People become less adventurous as they become older, the theory goes, and realize that they won't live forever.

Cohort theorists, on the other hand, believe quite the opposite. They maintain that in today's world (at least in North America), the life experiences you have from the ages of sixteen to twenty-one shape most of your values—for the rest of your life. If you rode a motorcycle when you were twenty, you'll still be doing it at fifty. If you were very spiritual in your late teens, you will be for the rest of your life. If you liked to take personal-life chances in your youth, you'll still be taking chances when you're older.

In truth, we are all probably an amalgam of both views, with some things about ourselves changing according to age and others not. It does appear, though, that the cohort effect is stronger today than in previous centuries. And it's certain that marketers strongly believe in its hypothesis. Just watch TV . . .

Some Key Niches

In every business, certain niches demand special attention. We've already examined one of them in Chapter 4: the upscale market. Here are four other segments that dominate travel thinking and buying, with key trends and hot buttons that appeal to each.

The Family Market   Family travel is big business. But it isn't like those old sitcoms. Today, 25 percent of all families are nontraditional: single-parent families, cohabitating parents, and multi-generational families are increasingly common. Family travel used to take place mostly during summers or at holidays. Today, nontraditional school calendars and the willingness of many parents to take their children out of school at any time of the year for a vacation has somewhat smoothed out the yearly peaks and valleys of family travel. Remember, too, that a child's opinions have a major influence on the family vacation decision.

Families look for a wide spectrum of activities that can keep both parents and kids occupied. Price and value are critical factors, as are lodging roominess, kid-friendly menus, and the accessibility of "instant playmates"—friends and supervision for the children. And don't forget another subsector of family travel: family reunions.

Romantic Travel   Romance is the fuel that fires much of vacation travel: Honeymoons, wedding anniversaries, vow renewals, or couples just wanting quality time together represent a remarkably lucrative opportunity.

Romantic travelers are willing to pay far more for a romantic holiday than they would for another kind of trip. (In fact, according to *Modern Bride* magazine, honeymooners typically spend two to three times more.) Romantics want to experience luxury, pampering, and self-indulgence. They love all-inclusive packages—the last thing they want is to worry about details.

Romantic travelers also like to get away from it all, usually in a tropical setting. (Hawaii and the Caribbean are the world's top two destinations for honeymooners.) They like to feel that they're in their own little private environment, with minimal interaction with others.

NICHES, NICHES, NICHES

Here are just some of the special interests to which travel can be tied (and, yes, some are quite odd).

Aerobics
Anthropology
Antiques
Archaeology/paleontology/history
Architecture
Art/painting/art history
Astrology
Astronomy
Backpacking
Ballooning
Barge/canal cruising
Baseball
Basketball
Bed & breakfasts/historic inns
Bicycle touring
Birdwatching
Brewery/beer festivals/winery tours
Bungee jumping
Butterflies/lepidoptery
Camel safaris
Camping
Canoeing/kayaking
Castles/palaces
Cattle driving
Cave art
Caving (spelunking)
Chauffeured tours
Chocolate tours
Christmas tours
Conservation
Cooking schools
Country houses/cottages/bungalows
Crafts tours
Cultural expeditions
Desert expeditions
Design tours
Disabled travelers
Diving
Doctors' tours
Dogsledding
Dude ranch/farmstays
Ecology/ecotourism
Ethnic tours
Executive/corporate fitness
Families
Festival tours

Fishing
Flightseeing
Foliage tours
Four-wheel drive
Gambling
Garden tours/horticulture
Gay tours
Gem collecting
Genealogy
Geology
Glacier tours/flights
Gold panning
Golf
Gourmet/gastronomy
Grandparent/grandchild tours
Hang gliding/soaring/paragliding
Health & fitness
Heli-rafting/skiing/trekking
Helicopter tours
Hiking/trekking/walking
Historic houses
Holistic health
Home stays/exchanges
Honeymoons
Horse packing/trekking
Horse racing
Houseboating
Ice climbing
Investment tours
Jeep safaris
Jungle expeditions/lodges
Kite flying
Kosher tours
Language study
Legend tours/literary tours
Llama packing
Marine biology
Martial arts
Medical services
Military history
Motorcamping
Motorcycle touring
Mountain bicycling
Mountaineering/rock climbing
Museum tours
Music/dance/opera

Mystery tours
National Park tours
Natural history
Nature trips
Nonsmokers tours
Nudist resorts/cruises
Nurses
Outdoor skills schools
Overlanding
Photographic tours
Police tours
Porcelain/china/pottery
Psychology/psychiatry
Quilting
Railway trips
Rainforest tours
Religion/spirituality/pilgrimages
Retreats/conferences
River rafting
Rollerblading
Running/jogging
RV rentals
Safaris
Sailing schools
School visits
Sea kayaking
Shopping
Single travelers
Skiing: cross-country/downhill
Skydiving
Snowmobiling
Snowshoeing
Soccer
Spa/hot springs
Sports tours
Stress management
Student tours/teachers tours
Study tours
Summer camps
Super Bowl/Rose Bowl

Surfing
Swimming
Tennis
Theater
Treasure hunting
Vegetarian tours
Veterans reunions
Videography tours
Villa/chateau rentals
Vintage cars
Volcano tours
Waterskiing/jet boating/jetskiing
Weddings
Weekend escapes
Whalewatching
Wilderness courses/lodges
Wildflower viewing
Wildlife viewing
Windjamming
Windsurfing
Women's tours
Writing workshops
Yoga/meditation
Youth tours
Zoology

Observing wildlife is a key goal for travelers on safari to an exotic location. (*Photo by Marc Mancini*)

Based on the earlier description of romantic travelers, which of the following do you think would appeal most to them? Check all that apply:

❏ A cruise
❏ An escorted tour
❏ An all-inclusive resort
❏ A convention
❏ A train voyage in Asia
❏ A trip through Europe in a rental RV

❏ An independent fly-drive tour
❏ A trip to Walt Disney World
❏ A stay at a condo or time-share
❏ A spa
❏ A day-long balloon ride
❏ A multi-day hiking expedition

Enrichment/Learning Travel   A significant number of people travel primarily to become more knowledgeable, to learn things, to enrich their lives. What are they drawn to? Tours and cruises that stress education (e.g., those with expert lecturers) appeal strongly to them. They love exotic, off-the-beaten-path destinations (like Easter Island or the Galapagos Islands) or places that offer rich cultural possibilities (e.g., Europe). Orlando, Branson, Las Vegas—these are the kinds of places they usually avoid. They like casual travel: Eddie Bauer, not Givenchy, is their style. They appreciate authentic experiences and aren't ostentatious—simple, even spartan accommodations are usually fine with them (even if they're well-off). And they love being with people just like them.

THE PLOG CONTINUUM

One of the most illuminating ways to understand travel consumer motivations is something called the Plog Continuum.

Analyst Stanley Plog argues that you can plot all travelers on a continuum scale, with "dependables" on one extreme and "venturers" on the other. Most people fall somewhere in between, with elements of both tendencies in varying proportions.

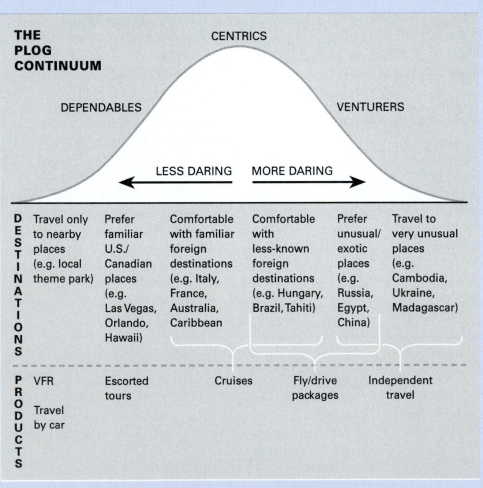

(Courtesy of Stanley C. Plog, Ph.D.)

Extreme dependables are cautious, even fearful of new experiences. Travel frightens them—indeed, they rarely go anywhere. To them, a drive to a nearby lake is an adventure.

Far more numerous are *regular dependables*. They do like travel, but only if it feels relatively safe. They do a lot of VFR travel (visiting with friends and relatives) and prefer their own car, mobile home, SUV or van to a plane, ship or motorcoach. Those who break from the VFR pattern favor tours, cruises and all-inclusives—these play to their concerns about safety, convenience, and ease. They love familiar, mass-market places, like Orlando, Las Vegas, national parks and English-speaking foreign destinations, such as Canada, Great Britain, and Australia.

On the opposite end of the scale are *extreme venturers*. These people are daring. They seek exotic, bold, even dangerous destinations and activities. They like to "discover" unusual places, are among the first to take up new, often extreme sports and see physical and cultural challenges as keenly attractive. They travel a lot—but rarely purchase their travel through conventional suppliers or travel agents. (They're too independent for that.)

Regular venturers are less bold, but are still more daring than most. They welcome unusual cultural experiences and prefer independent trips. When they take a tour or a cruise, it's to places like Africa, South America, or Asia, and with a travel company that understands their distinct needs.

Most consumers fall towards the middle of Plog's Continuum. (These he calls *centrists*.) How about you? In the space below, write whether you'd consider yourself an extreme dependable, regular dependable, centrist, regular venturer, or extreme venturer. Explain why.

The Adventure Market   Somewhat similar to the enrichment market is the adventure niche. These travelers also like to learn and prefer unusual destinations. They, too, don't usually need luxury, even if they can afford it.

The big difference, however, is that adventurers *place a distinct emphasis on being active*. They want to challenge the environment they're in. Hiking, cross-country skiing, diving, whitewater river rafting—these are the kinds of things they want to do. They like to learn new skills or to do what they do at home, but in new surroundings.

The adventure market is usually divided into two categories: **soft adventure** and **hard adventure.** Soft adventure travelers like to do things that reasonably fit people can achieve. Hard adventure travelers prefer more extreme activities. It's the difference between snorkelers and deep-sea divers, hikers and mountain-climbers.

Generational Selling and Marketing

Sales and marketing specialists not only adjust their products and approach to special interests, but also to cohorts. Most demographers divide today's consumers into five groups:

- Seniors (born 1935 or earlier)
- The Swing Generation (born 1936–1945)
- Baby Boomers (born 1946–1963)
- Generation X (born 1964–1975)
- Echo Boomers (born 1976 or later)

Of these, the Baby Boomer generation seems to attract the most attention. The reason: Baby Boomers are currently passing though their middle-age period, when their disposable income is highest and when their schedules are becoming more flexible. Soon they'll reach retirement age and travel even more. There are about 70 million Baby Boomers in the United States alone—their sheer numbers demand attention.

What do Baby Boomers prefer in travel? They like independent tours and the semi-structure of certain cruise experiences. Stress-relief, pampering, ecology, and excellence are strong hot buttons for them. They consider health, fitness, and learning to be important travel goals.

And what of the other major cohorts?

- **Seniors** tend to favor familiar, domestic destinations. They like structured travel products (like escorted tours and cruises) with all-day planned activities. They're very safety-conscious and are drawn to bargains.
- **The Swing Generation** are somewhat similar to the Seniors, but favor *value* over price. They're somewhat more open to soft adventure and foreign destinations, and seek out learning opportunities.
- **Generation Xers** are far more adventurous and many seek out "extreme" activities. They're ecologically conscious and favor independent, flexible travel. They're somewhat cynical about marketing messages, yet are attracted to high-profile, well-known travel brands.
- **Echo Boomers** are attracted to fun, active travel environments. They like meeting people of their own age, look for novelty, seek value and favor well-known, mass-market destinations. Like Baby Boomers, they like pampering and independence.

Remember, the above generational profiles reflect trends and are built on generalities. Within each cohort are plenty of people whose wants and needs are not typical of their age peers.

SELLING CORPORATE TRAVEL

This book has focused almost exclusively on leisure travel. But what about business travelers? What are their needs? And how can you best satisfy them?

If you've ever traveled for business, think of two ways business travel is a positive experience and two ways it's negative. If you've never traveled for business, try to imagine its benefits and drawbacks. Write your answers below:

Positive   *Negative*

1.   1.

2.   2.

Which column was the easiest to fill? Probably the negative one. Because, on the surface, the negative aspects of business travel dominate:

- It's highly stressful (lonely hotel rooms, long flights in narrow seats, wild cab journeys, etc.)
- It separates you from your home life
- It often goes unappreciated by management

Yet there are positive aspects, too:

- It enables you to do business more directly and personally
- It could lead to "add-on" leisure opportunities (e.g., an extra day in New York City for sightseeing)
- It may satisfy a need to get away from the regular routines of home life

But how do sales and service skills contribute to the corporate travel experience? To answer this question, you must understand how business travel is managed.

Two paradigms mark the world of corporate travel:

1. **A company has its own internal travel department:** A team of travel professionals, headed by a corporate travel manager, makes travel arrangements for the company's employees. Or . . .

2. **A company makes most or all of its travel arrangements through a travel agency,** either as part of a formal relationship between the two businesses or, informally, with individuals arranging things with agencies of their choice.

HOW CAN A TRAVEL AGENCY SELL ITSELF TO CORPORATE CLIENTS?

A travel agency can best secure corporate business by pitching the following:

1. Emphasize that you understand the specific needs of the corporate traveler.
2. Promise that you will arrange travel efficiently, swiftly, and within corporate travel policy. (Businesses usually set clear limits on which suppliers its employees can use and which cost guidelines must be met.)
3. Describe the success you've had serving other companies. Emphasize your positive track record.
4. Assure them that specific agents will be assigned to serve their account, so both sides can become familiar with each other's needs.
5. Promise that you'll do all you can to search out the best prices possible, thus helping them in their efforts to contain costs.
6. Explain that you can also help their employees with their leisure trips, as well as perhaps assist with meeting planning, if the need arises.

Meeting the Corporate Traveler's Needs

Three factors affect a business travelers' experience. Here's how to address those factors:

1. Unlike vacationers, **many business travelers perceive travel as a necessary evil.** To soften the experience, a travel professional should, in any way possible, reduce unknowns and facilitate the trip.
2. **Business travelers**—if they have the time—**like to profit from the potential leisure-like benefits of their trip.** Book a hotel with a view, suggest a sight to see in their free time, inform them of a special restaurant for that after-hours meal.
3. **Business travelers use travel to achieve recognition.** Frequent-flyer upgrades to first class, prearranged transfers or concierge-level hotel rooms play to the road warrior's desire to be recognized and rewarded for the stress they must endure.

SELLING TO GROUPS

Do you belong to any groups? Think hard. You may be associated with more than you think. For example, do you get mailings from your high school alumni association? There's one example. Write down as many groups as you can think of that you're in some way connected to:

The kinds of groups you've probably just listed are called affinity groups. **Affinity groups are groups distinguished by their common interest and/or history of shared activities.** The beauty of selling to such groups: It requires only somewhat more work than selling to an individual—the time-profit equation is superb. You can also arrange what's called a **speculative group,** one where **you build a group departure around a niche or theme** (e.g., a museum tour) **and offer it to the public.** Tour operators, cruise lines and hotels are the most eager among suppliers to serve group needs.

Several fine books are available that explain, in detail, how to target, market, and sell to groups. Let's limit ourselves, then, to a few of the most valuable insights on this approach to travel sales:

- **Understand your group's needs.** You must sell to a group in much the same way as you do to an individual: Assess its needs, design a trip to meet those needs, use benefits language, etc. Also, integrate the generic benefits of group travel into your promotional efforts: time and money savings, freedom from hassles, learning opportunities, and the companionship of people with similar interests.
- **If possible, find a "pied piper."** A pied piper is a member of a group, club or organization who helps promote a tour to the group, usually in return for a free trip. Identify a leader of the affinity group who is enthusiastic, persuasive, and well known to the group. Two obvious examples: a church's minister or a school's teacher. For speculative groups, the pied piper is often a public figure (e.g., a disc jockey).
- **Stage a group night.** Invite all those interested to attend a presentation about your special departure. Be prepared to offer them an incentive (e.g., an upgraded stateroom or $200 discount) if they sign up then and there.
- **Get the supplier to offer support.** If you're at an agency, cruise lines, tour operators and all-inclusive resorts sometimes agree to provide monies to subsidize your promotion. It's called co-op money. The support can also take the form of free tour manager tickets, tote bags and/or shells as a basis for your brochure. (**Shells are preprinted flyers or brochures with photos and graphics, but with large blank spaces.** You have your own text printed in the blank spaces; the surrounding full-color artwork makes your promotional piece look highly professional.)
- **Make sure you're covered by insurance.** Usually the supplier's or agency's insurance will cover you, but be certain that's true for your group departure.

Incentive Groups

One very specialized form of group business: **incentives.** The word *incentive* can be used to describe **any program that uses an awards system to improve work performance.**

Some examples: A $5,000 bonus for all insurance representatives who beat their yearly quotas by 10 percent; a free stereo system for a car salesperson who sells more than forty cars in six months; a free health club membership to every worker in a plant where no industrial accidents occur during the year.

Travel is one of the most popular awards for incentive programs. That's why so many travel providers pursue group incentive business. Incentive clients want and will pay for the best travel experience possible. (It's dogma among incentive companies that an award must be superior, distinctive, and dramatic.) Most of all, it's a win-win situation for everyone: The incentive operator makes money (the net profit margin is typically 15 to 30 percent), the company that's the client for the incentive makes more profits (its employees are "incentivized" to perform better), and the salesperson gets a great trip with other winners from the company (reinforcing each other's success).

The incentive business is a highly specialized one, with very much its own rules for promoting and operating group departures.

WRITING THAT SELLS

Do you have to be a gifted writer to sell, market, and serve your customers? Perhaps not. But to be a respected professional in sales, service and, certainly, marketing, you must know how to write clear, concise, and persuasive prose. And if you wish to rise through the ranks of the travel industry, writing skills are a *must*.

Try listing five sales, service and/or marketing activities that would require solid writing skills. We'll help you get started with the first one:

1. *Sending e-mail to clients about a great new deal you're offering*.
2.

3.

4.

5.

As your list proves, writing skills are important to many travel-related activities. So here are seven strategies that you can apply to power up your prose.

1. Be Correct

It's absolutely essential that your spelling be perfect and your grammar correct. Customers, fellow workers, and those at other companies will judge your professionalism by how correctly you write. Do spell *and* grammar checks on everything you write, *then* reread what you've written. (Errors *can* slip by computer checks.) If it's something really important, also have a colleague go over what you've written.

2. Streamline Your Style

Many people feel that to impress, they must write long, complicated sentences and use esoteric words. Wrong. This isn't literature; it's business or promotional writing. Simple and direct work much better, plus you have less of a chance of making a mistake.

3. Use Contractions

Did a teacher once tell you that skilled writers avoid contractions, like *it's*, *let's* or *can't*? Forget it. Your writing should mirror the way you talk. Even the most literate people today use contractions all the time.

4. Choose Words, Phrases, and Sentences That Link You to the Reader

Readers like to feel that they're being spoken to. Questions ("Why this offer?"), commands ("Take advantage of our offer now") and the words *we* and *you* (and all their variants, like *yours, our,* etc.) forge a bond between writer and reader.

5. Avoid Negatives

Sometimes you can't avoid them (like just now), but too many negative phrases undermine the positive tone your prose should convey. As you learned in Chapter 5, this rule applies to verbal statements, too. Positive language is a cornerstone of quality service, sales and marketing. Try turning these negative sentences into positives. We've started you off with an example:

Negative	*Positive*
1. *Tour brochure*: You shouldn't take this tour without buying travel insurance. It isn't too expensive, either.	*Protect your tour investment by taking out travel insurance. We've made it quite affordable for you.*

2. *Hotel front desk sign*: Guests can't be checked in until 4 PM. They won't be ready until then.

3. *Memo to staff*: Don't keep looking down when a client walks in.

4. *Cruise ad*: Don't choose a cruise line that doesn't understand what your family wants.

5. *Proposal to group for an affinity tour*: Your members won't be disappointed that our prices won't be high.

Now check the alternatives you wrote. Almost certainly they feel more positive. Did you also use any of the writing tactics we've discussed, like using connecting words? All the better. Here are more tips:

6. Replace Passive Constructions with Active Ones

A passive construction is one in which the subject (usually one of the first words) *receives* the action, rather than performs it. Passive constructions rob your prose of energy and directness. Consider this extreme example: Should it be: "Your travel dreams are made to come true by us" or "We make your travel dreams come true"? The right choice should be obvious.

7. Edit

Ever walk out of a theater and say: "That movie could have been a half-hour shorter!" Blame the director and the editor, who felt that their film *had to* have all those wonderful scenes they shot. Blame yourself, too, if your brochure has so many words that you must use a teeny typeface to get them all in.

The Gettysburg Address contains 246 words, the Lord's Prayer 56, and one of drama's most striking lines, "To be or not to be," a mere 6. Does that marketing plan of yours really need 10,000?

ADJUSTING TO CHALLENGING TIMES

Normally, if you have a strong commitment to and vision for your travel product, then sales, service, and marketing success will come easy. But there are times—challenging times—when success, and profits, become more elusive.

A weak economy is one example. When unemployment is high and money is tight, people begin to cut back on their discretionary purchases. Travel is one such non-essential. In such cases, deep discounting along with internal cost-cutting, enables travel providers to stimulate sales and—hopefully—at least break even. The idea: to position your product and strengthen your brand so that when the economic recovery occurs, you'll be well set for success.

Also, certain sectors of travel seem immune to recession. Since recession is often accompanied by a deflated currency value, this may actually help inbound tourism from other countries. For example, when the U.S. dollar is weak, foreigners find travel to America an attractive value. (Conversely, when the dollar is strong, outbound U.S. tourism to other countries increases.) Also, value-priced hotels and motels do well during a recession, as do close-to-home, drive-to attractions.

Some also argue that luxury products continue to do well, too, since the wealthy are relatively immune to negative financial forces. But it depends. Products that cater to older affluent travelers do hold up, since their relatively safe investments and "I may only a have a few healthy years left" attitude prevail. Younger affluent customers, however, are more sensitive to a recession, since their wealth tends to be tied up in more risky investments. If your "paper wealth" (e.g., stocks) tumbles, you're not exactly ready to spend a lot on travel.

Economic turbulence, however, always gives way to better times. Indeed, many fortunes were made by people who invested in travel when the business seemed at its worst.

A more troubling event is terrorism. When a terrorist act takes place, travel usually shrinks, especially if the event had anything to do with tourism. Here's what you must keep in mind when a terrorist act occurs. To some extent, the following also apply to natural disasters, like earthquakes and hurricanes:

1. **The consumer's response is irrational.** The reasons people cease to travel have little to do with logic. For example, on 9/11/01, more peo-

ple died in automobile accidents in America than in the four hijacked aircraft. Yet people abandoned flying for drive vacations instead. After the 1989 Oakland/San Francisco earthquake, tourism to the Bay Area plummeted, even though the likelihood of another major earthquake was remote.

2. **The response is based on an individual's "risk quotient."** Adventurous travelers are the quickest to travel again, timid ones the slowest. Honeymooners, the physically challenged, and, to some extent, families resist the downturn better than do others.

3. **The booking window shortens.** This is especially true with terrorism. Instead of planning their trips months out, consumers tend toward last-minute buying (e.g., thirty days out).

4. **The effect diminishes as you distance yourself from the perceived danger.** The 1991 Gulf War extinguished travel in the Middle East, but it also hurt travel somewhat in Europe, Morocco, and parts of Asia. The effect was less severe in Latin America, Australia, and North America.

5. **The response will be temporary.** A recovery usually begins about three months after the event, picks up momentum around six months out, and usually approaches ninety percent of previous tourism within a year.

Name: _____   Date: _____

ACTIVITY #1   RATING A WEB SITE

In Chapter 1 you analyzed three Web sites. Now let's refine your analytical skills even more. Select any travel site. Circle one grade for each question, according to the criteria given. Be prepared to explain your assessment.

Web site chosen: _____

1. Does it encourage a "relationship"?	A	B	C	D	F	NA
2. Is it entertaining?	A	B	C	D	F	NA
3. Is simplicity a characteristic?	A	B	C	D	F	NA
4. Is it user-friendly?	A	B	C	D	F	NA
5. Does it customize to the user's interests?	A	B	C	D	F	NA
6. Is it interactive?	A	B	C	D	F	NA
7. Does it facilitate buying?	A	B	C	D	F	NA
8. Is it free of errors?	A	B	C	D	F	NA
9. Does it provide rich information?	A	B	C	D	F	NA
10. Is it up-to-date?	A	B	C	D	F	NA

Other comments:

Name: _____ Date: _____

ACTIVITY #2 ANALYZING GOOD WRITING

Below is the promotional description from a brochure. Analyze its prose. Cite any examples of the seven writing strategies cited in this chapter. Indicate any other examples of especially effective writing tactics you find. Is there anything you'd rewrite?

Join Pastor Trent Jones and your fellow congregation members on an unusual, interesting and port-intensive cruise itinerary to San Juan, St. Thomas, St. Maarten, Dominica, Barbados and Martinique. And there is no better way to do this than on an Acme cruise.

We will fly on Friday, May 29, to San Juan. After an overnight stay at a fine San Juan hotel, a Saturday tour of historic Old San Juan will take place, with plenty of time for shopping, too. The group will board the cruise ship that evening. Then it will be five good ports in a row.

No one will want to miss St. Thomas, our first port, with so many things to be done there. The next day it will be St. Maarten, an island that some consider to be the most satisfying island in the Caribbean. Onward to Dominica, with many rivers, a famous grotto and the only remaining Carib Indians anywhere. Then Barbados, with many natural wonders to be seen. Following this is Martinique, with the most French ambiance found in the Caribbean.

Afterward it's a day at sea and, on our final day, a return to San Juan, with many new memories that you will never forget.

Name: _____   Date: _____

ACTIVITY #2   CONTINUED

Examples of seven writing strategies:

Other tactics used (give examples):

Anything you'd rewrite? How would you rephrase it?

Name: _____   Date: _____

ACTIVITY #3   WHO TARGETS NICHES?

Below are a series of niches, some of which we've examined, some we haven't. Using the Internet or other resources, find one supplier that clearly targets the niche given. It can be a hotel, tour operator, cruise line, attraction, or other travel supplier. Give a very brief description of the product that supplier provides.

Niche	**Supplier's name/category**	**Description of product**
Example: Families	Disney Cruise Line	Ships with numerous activities/areas for various child age groups. Adult-exclusive areas/activities, too.

1. Families

2. Romantics

3. Enrichment/learning

4. Adventurers

5. Seniors (over 65)

6. The affluent

7. Wine connoisseurs

8. Golfers

8

Your Future in Sales, Service, and Marketing

OBJECTIVES

After reading this chapter, you'll be able to:

- Launch and build a career in travel

- Motivate staff to sell

- Adjust and prepare for future trends in travel sales, service and marketing

Is travel like other businesses? Are its career paths clearly marked? What happens when you get to the management level? And what does the future hold for the travel industry? This chapter will answer these questions, and more.

LAUNCHING AND BUILDING YOUR CAREER

Let's assume you're thinking about a career in travel sales, service or marketing. What would be your dream job? Write it here.

Now list the three things about yourself that you feel would make you successful in your dream career:

1.

2.

3.

Let's review what the experts say about the skills you'll need in the travel business. Compare them with your list.

Traits for Travel

What would it take for you to be a success in travel service and sales?

You must be **positive** and **energetic,** since travel (especially leisure travel) should be an exciting and pleasurable experience. You need to convey that to your customers and to your fellow professionals. Such confidence is invaluable, especially during trying times such as those that occurred after the terrorist attacks of September 11, 2001.

You must also be **efficient.** Travel often requires the ability to choreograph many components into a satisfying experience. You need to be **persuasive, convincing,** and **believe in** the quality of what you sell. You must have a strong sense of **ethics,** since the opportunity to take advantage of travelers occurs frequently in certain sectors of the travel business.

Commitment is critical, as well: to your fellow employees, to your customers and to your overall job. As with any employment, you need to have good work habits: **Punctuality,** a **professional image** and a desire to **serve** your clients' needs are all essential. In some jobs you need to **love to travel;** in others you must at least convey a love of travel to those whom you counsel. You should have a natural **curiosity** about the products and places that shape the travel experience. **Foreign language skills** are a plus in many sectors. Lastly, you must **appreciate people.** For they are the reason you have your job.

SPECIFIC CAREERS IN TRAVEL

Here's a list of travel-related jobs that require sales, service, or marketing skills, either to-the-public, business-to-business, or within-business.

AIRLINES

The airline industry is one of the largest sectors in travel. It's made up of hundreds of airlines worldwide, both big and small, and the companies that support them.

- Senior executives, directors, and managers
- Reservationists
- Ticketing / gate agents
- Customer service representatives
- District sales representatives
- Flight attendants
- Rate desk agents
- Human resources / training specialists
- Security / safety personnel

AIRPORT OPERATIONS

A vast array of personnel ensures that airports operate efficiently, safely and profitably.

- Senior executives, directors, and managers
- Human resources / training specialists
- Immigration / customs personnel
- Security / safety personnel
- Retail sales and management (e.g., food concessions, stores, duty-free outlet, etc.)

CAR RENTAL COMPANIES

About a half-dozen huge companies dominate this industry, with hundreds of thousands employed worldwide. Locations are most often at airports, but center-city locations are also common.

- Senior executives, directors, and managers
- Reservationists
- Counter sales agents
- District sales managers
- Human resources / training specialists
- Shuttle drivers

CONVENTIONS AND MEETINGS

This is a highly diversified sector, with convention centers, hotels, visitors bureaus, meeting planners, transportation providers, and the like all working together to facilitate conferences, board meetings, sales meetings, trade shows, educational sessions, workshops, exhibits, and much more.

- Senior executives, directors, and managers
- Meeting planners
- Food and beverage staff
- Sales representatives
- Shipping specialists

(continued)

SPECIFIC CAREERS IN TRAVEL *(CONTINUED)*

CORPORATE TRAVEL MANAGEMENT

Most companies and organizations have employees who travel a great deal. To purchase and coordinate their travel, most large businesses have staff—headed by corporate travel managers—to oversee travel. At some companies, travel management is outsourced to travel agencies.

- Senior executives, directors, and managers
- Human resources / training specialists
- Corporate travel managers
- Travel agents
- Account managers

CRUISE INDUSTRY

The cruise industry is one of travel's fastest growing sectors. It's divided into two large groups: onboard and land-based. In addition to the megaships and companies that operate them, there are also many niche cruise companies: small, education-oriented vessels, masted sailing ships, riverboats, sightseeing vessels, boat charters, etc.

- Senior executives, directors, and managers
- Reservationists
- Human resources / training specialists
- Shipboard executives, support staff, and entertainers
- District sales managers
- Port staff
- Shore excursion personnel
- Passenger service representatives
- Safety / security specialists

INCENTIVE TRAVEL

In many businesses, travel is awarded to those who excel in on-job performance, sales, safety, etc. This is called incentive travel. Many tour-like companies specialize in designing, coordinating, operating, and bringing an entertaining and motivational touch to incentive travel events.

- Senior executives, directors, and managers
- Clerical support
- Event planners
- Trip directors
- Supplier coordinators
- Sales representatives
- Audio-visual / graphics specialists

LODGING INDUSTRY

The lodging industry is huge, with millions of job positions worldwide. Included in this category are numerous subdivisions: resorts, all-suite hotels, bed-and-breakfasts, spas, inns, hostels, RV campgrounds, ski resorts, etc.

- Senior executives, directors, and managers
- Reservationists
- Front desk staff
- Food and beverage staff
- Concierges
- Business center staff
- Human resources / training specialists
- Audio-visual coordinators
- Groups / meetings coordinators
- Safety / security specialists
- Sales representatives

MOTORCOACH OPERATORS

The motorcoach industry is a large one in America, with hundreds of local operators and several large regional or national ones. Tours, charters, and local transportation make up the bulk of the business. There is a major, nationwide demand for motorcoach drivers.

- Senior executives, directors, and managers
- Sales representatives
- Reservationists
- Dispatchers / schedulers
- Tour guides
- Tour conductors

ON-LINE TRAVEL PROVIDERS

It seems clear that much travel in the future will be bought on-line, either directly from suppliers (e.g., the airlines) or through "virtual" travel agencies and providers. Growth will be especially strong where a travel commodity (e.g., an airline ticket) is involved, less so when the travel product is a more complex experience (e.g., a tour).

- Senior executives, directors, and managers
- Sales representatives
- Travel agents
- Automation specialists
- Webmasters

RAIL TRAVEL

Train travel is projected to grow in the United States and it's already a major transportation choice in other countries. There are also "private" trains that carry tourists on scenic trips, sometimes for an hour or two, sometimes for thousands of miles.

- Senior executives, directors, and managers
- District sales representatives
- Human resources / training specialists
- Ticketing agents
- Onboard attendants

RESEARCH & MARKETING COMPANIES

Several companies specialize in gathering and analyzing travel data. They are often commissioned by industry organizations, but individual companies also hire them to provide proprietary insights into the travel patterns of their customers. Other companies (e.g., advertising agencies) specialize in applying this information to marketing and promotional campaigns.

- Senior executives, directors, and managers
- Statistical analysts / forecasters
- Writers / photographers

THEME PARKS

Theme parks have become major forces in the travel industry, most especially in Florida and California. The largest ones also sell full travel packages (hotel, transportation, air, and admissions) to the public.

- Senior executives, directors, and managers
- Admissions agents
- Ride operators
- Food service personnel
- Tour guides
- Sales representatives
- Public relations specialists
- Security / safety personnel

(continued)

SPECIFIC CAREERS IN TRAVEL *(CONTINUED)*

TOUR OPERATORS

The tour industry is divided into many sub-categories: local sightseeing tours, escorted motorcoach tours, independent tours, incentive trips, travel clubs, etc. In North America, independent "fly-drive" tours are the most popular, whereas inclusive, escorted tours are most popular abroad.

- Senior executives, directors, and managers
- Reservationists
- Tour conductors
- Tour guides
- District sales managers
- Human resources / training specialists
- Tour planners

TRADE ASSOCIATIONS

Every sector of the travel industry has at least one trade association that represents its interests. Trade associations can do any or all of the following: host trade shows, conduct research projects, lobby for the industry, conduct public relation campaigns, obtain legal advice for members, sponsor publications, raise funds, and provide training events and tools.

- Senior executives, directors, and managers
- Research staff
- Writers
- Educational specialists / trainers
- Research analysts
- Meeting planners
- Publication editors
- Lobbyists
- Public relations specialists

TRAVEL AGENCY OPERATIONS

Travel agencies continue to book the majority of travel in North America, including 80–90 percent of all packaged travel, 65 percent of air tickets and 25 percent of lodging. The industry is moving away from its mom-and-pop profile to one where megachains and consortia of independent agencies dominate.

- Senior executives, directors, managers, owners
- Human resources / training specialists
- Travel agents (leisure and/or corporate)
- Outside sales representatives
- Cruise, groups, destination, corporate travel specialists
- Group specialists
- Vendor negotiators

TRAVEL PUBLICATIONS

Dozens of periodicals, both for consumers and for industry professionals, provide information and analysis of travel and tourism trends. Others (e.g., newspapers), have columns that focus on travel. It's a myth that travel publications seek out the work of freelance travel writers. There are also thousands of travel books and Web sites that require the skills of travel writers. You must have a strong publication track record before your work will be considered. Most of this kind of work is done by staff writers or very well-known freelancers.

- Senior executives, directors, and managers
- Sales representatives
- Reporters / writers
- Editors
- Graphics artists
- Sales representatives
- Meeting planners

VISITOR BUREAUS

Most cities, regions, states and countries have organizations that help attract visitors and groups, and represent those businesses that cater to them. These are called visitors bureaus, tourist bureaus, or destination marketing organizations (DMOs).

- Senior executives, directors, and managers
- Marketing coordinators
- Special events coordinators
- Public information officers
- Photographers

SUPPORT INDUSTRIES

Many companies provide support to the travel industry in important ways, including credit card providers, legal firms, training companies, insurance companies, food service providers, and advertising / PR firms.

(Courtesy of the Hogan Family Foundation)

Nuts and Bolts

How do you get that first sales or service travel job? Here's what you must do:

1. **Create a professional resumé and cover letter.** The personnel director will use it as a "snapshot" of your capabilities.
2. **Interact with as many travel professionals as you can.** Attending travel industry events and joining travel-related organizations will provide important contacts and perhaps a mentor.
3. **Get an interview.** Interviews are somewhat more important in travel than in other industries. The reason: People skills are so essential to the travel business. Many interviewers feel that they can best assess a potential employee's people skills through an interview. Do all you can to get some time with the person who hires for a company and stress the traits and skills we cited earlier.
4. **Cite prior experience.** Unfortunately, the travel industry tends to favor hiring people with prior experience in its field. To circumvent this, underscore those skills you acquired elsewhere (e.g., regular contact with customers, with many upsell opportunities) and express your conviction that you can translate these to your new travel career.
5. **Be flexible.** Travel jobs often entail unconventional schedules, an ability to respond nimbly to all sorts of situations, and a willingness to perform beyond the boundaries of a job description.
6. **Follow up.** Many employers in the travel business actually like an applicant to follow up regularly on job opportunities. They see it as a reflection of desire, perseverance, enthusiasm, and commitment.

JOB AVAILABILITY

The most in-demand career in travel is probably that of **tour manager. (A person who accompanies, entertains, manages, and narrates multiday tours.)** Most large tour companies have twenty-five to thirty applicants for each tour manager they hire. Also relatively hard to get are flight attendant jobs, supplier rep jobs, and certain positions on cruise ships, such as **cruise director. (The person who coordinates most informational and entertainment activities on the cruise.)**

On the other hand, hotel front-line service positions are quite easy to obtain, especially if you have the right personality. The easiest to get: airport jobs, especially in security, and food services. Pay in these careers is low, the demands high, and the location not always desirable. As a result, turnover is rapid and employers find it a challenge to hire good employees. But remember: A person who performs well in the travel business often gets rapid promotions.

Unique Aspects of Travel Careers

Certain trends are more obvious in travel than in others:

- **As we hinted above, advancement from front-line positions to middle management is rapid.** It's common to become a front-desk manager in a few years, for a tour manager to obtain an executive position within five or six, and for travel agents, if they're with a big company, to have rapid salary advancement.
- **Senior management often worked their way up from front-line positions, too.** The current president of AAA—a huge, multifaceted organization—began by driving a roadside emergency tow-truck. The senior vice president of the world's largest cruise line, Carnival, was once a travel agent. The heads of several major tour operators started as tour managers. The president of a major movie studio (that offers tours on its lot) was once a tour guide there.
- **The travel industry is very "in-bred."** In most fields, it's common for someone to occupy a position with, say, Maxwell House Coffee, then take a better job with Dunlop Tires and end up at Motorola. This is much less common in travel, where lateral or upward career changes stay largely within the industry or even within industry sectors. That's why networking at all levels is essential.
- **There's a surprising camaraderie between travel professionals at competing companies.** In some industries, it's considered almost traitorous to socialize with the competition. Not so in travel (except perhaps among airline CEOs). Tour, cruise, and travel agency personnel are especially gracious to one another (perhaps because lateral company career moves are so common).
- **Within companies, there's a greater divide between sales/marketing professionals and operations.** This disconnect—a counterproductive phenomenon—sometimes leads to unkept consumer promises and frequent service breakdowns. Many hotels, for example, suffer from poor communication between, say, the sales department and the front desk.

- **The perks are sometimes wonderful.** Industry discounts are common and quite attractive compared to other businesses. Be careful, though: This should not be the primary reason you go into travel.

MOTIVATING STAFF TO SELL

Imagine that you've risen to the level of manager at a medium-size travel agency. How could you encourage your travel counselors to go beyond transactional service and selling to arrive at a genuine consultative approach? Write three strategies you would use:

1.

2.

3.

Sometimes motivation is simply a matter of giving clear directions, providing positive feedback, and treating employees well.

Here are five tactics that work in virtually every sales and service environment. Compare them with the ones you wrote.

1. Set Realistic and Measurable Goals

Should a car rental company ask employees to do double the work in the same amount of time? Should a cruise line tell a half-dozen dining room waiters to help every single guest with their buffet tray, even though hundreds pass through the service line every five minutes? Should a hotel manager tell her sales force that their revenue for the upcoming year should triple?

All of these goals would probably be impossible to achieve. Equally wrong is to set goals that have no *measurable* criteria. "I want us to do a much better job in the coming weeks" is fine, but how is "a much better job" or "coming weeks" to be measured?

2. Provide Monetary Incentives

At the very least, people should be compensated fairly for what's expected of them. Otherwise, their motivation will quickly evaporate. For most people, more is required: Achievable goals and subsequent performance can be directly tied to bonuses, incentives and/or commissions. Two travel industry examples:

- Many car rental companies reward airport counter sales personnel with commissions for each upgrade or cross-sell item (e.g., insurance) they sell.
- In the mid-1990s, the president of Continental Airlines—facing unacceptable service ratings and mounting revenue losses—promised employees cash bonuses for each month that Continental was rated among the top three airlines in on-time performance and luggage handling. The bonuses became bigger if Continental placed first. In less than sixty days, Continental went from the bottom of the airline ratings to the top.

3. Give Positive Reinforcement

Author Kenneth Blanchard put it this way: "You must catch people doing right." Applauding positive behavior is far more effective than criticizing negative habits. Surprisingly, study after study have indicated that non-monetary rewards (praise, a certificate, an employee of the month award, etc.) work almost as well and, in some cases, better than money.

What about criticism, discipline, and reprimands? Sometimes they're needed. Be aware, however, that though they may improve things temporarily, they'll do nothing for long-term motivation. And what about no feedback at all? Consider this: "Figure that you're doing your job well unless I tell you otherwise." How would you feel about that sentence if it were said to you? Describe your reaction below.

WHAT IS MOTIVATION?

One dictionary defines **motivation** as "an inner urge that prompts a person to act with a sense of purpose." A more pragmatic definition: **It's the process of getting people to do what you want them to do**. No matter how you look at it, improving sales, service and motivation usually requires changing habits, generally by replacing a counterproductive behavior with a better one. It also requires three assumptions:

- People generally want to do a good job.
- People want to have a good time while working.
- People want to give their best and be recognized for it.

So why doesn't everyone work in a motivated manner? Perhaps it's a matter of character—a set of personality traits so deeply imbedded that even enlightened direction can't change it. Often, though, people don't know *how* to do their job well—hence the need for constant, consistent training.

4. Listen to Employee Suggestions

Wise companies often say that their CEO isn't at the top.

At the top are customers, followed by front-line employees, management, *then* the CEO. It's front-liners who genuinely understand what should—and should not—be done. Managers must be open to employee suggestions—at the very least these ideas provide a window onto what employees and customers experience on a regular basis.

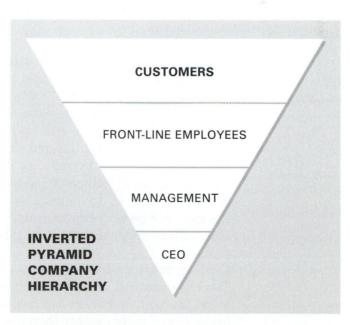

CUSTOMERS

FRONT-LINE EMPLOYEES

MANAGEMENT

CEO

**INVERTED
PYRAMID
COMPANY
HIERARCHY**

5. Set the Example

If you've ever been on an escorted tour, you've seen how most people look to others for direction. When the tour manager goes through one of five doors, so, too, will her entire group, even though four other doors are available. If group members hear her order meatloaf in a restaurant, most will also order meatloaf.

This same principle applies to managing motivation. If a supervisor greets people warmly, follows procedures thoroughly, is consistently helpful and remains enthused about work, then his employees will most likely be motivated to do the same.

THE FUTURE OF TRAVEL SALES, SERVICE, AND MARKETING

In the space below, list two products or services that almost no one had or used ten years ago, but that are relatively common today. They can be from any industry:

Amazing how quickly things change, isn't it? It will be equally amazing how things change in the next ten years. Almost surely these changes will affect—perhaps even transform—how you work, serve, market and/or sell.

Here are ten developments that are almost sure to take place in the travel industry:

1. **People will more often buy directly from suppliers.** Increased familiarity with the Internet and more sophisticated computer voice recognition programs will enable consumers to easily access information and buy products with no help from travel agents or other intermediaries. This isn't as bad as it sounds, though. Agents will focus less on commodities and more on experiences, where personal advice, opinion, and knowledge play a large part in customer choice. Upscale travelers will continue to use trusted agents to do what they don't have time to do themselves. The future of supplier reservationists may not be very bright, however. "Intelligent" programs will enable callers and computers to interact verbally for simple transactions.

2. **Cruises, tours, and all-inclusive resorts will continue to be popular.** Travel agents will recommend them and consumers will be drawn to them, if only to avoid on-trip hassles. These products will become formatted even more flexibly than they are today.

3. **Several popular destinations that you've never heard of will emerge.** In 1960, almost no one had heard of Orlando, Cancun, or

Branson. Twenty years from now, several places that, today, are largely unknown will be magnets for tourism.

4. **Family travel will decline.** Current demographic studies seem to indicate that fewer people will be having children in the next few years, leading to a slowdown in family travel. Family-oriented destinations and attractions will try to expand their appeal to other cohorts and lifestyles.

5. **Interactivity will dominate the media.** Digital cable and telephone lines will permit greater purchasing pattern analysis, increased program choices and narrowly focused customization. If you choose to watch (at any time of your choice) a movie set in Venice, the TV will detect your interest in Italy, then report it to suppliers-sponsors. The next day you'll receive an e-mail offer from an Italy specialist tour operator, a few days later a coupon from your local Olive Garden restaurant shows up in your mailbox, and who knows what else.

6. **Reservationists and travel agents will be on camera.** Go on the Internet, click on an icon for "personal help." A live person will appear on the screen to answer your questions (voice exchange will occur via a toll-free phone number). That "host" will show you video clips and personalize the sales experience. Only very service-oriented companies, however, will offer this feature. Others will try to automate the entire process, perhaps using "avatars" (animated, virtual reservationists that will appear on your computer monitor).

7. **Hotels will automate their services more completely.** The lodging industry finds it so hard to hire good people that it will replace many jobs with automated systems. As with airlines, you'll check in at a kiosk, where an always-friendly virtual receptionist will greet you and issue you your room key.

8. **Unexpected, worrisome events will continue to disrupt travel and interrupt industry progress.** Natural disasters, terrorist acts, and other unforeseen events are bound to occur. The travel industry is resilient, though. Indeed, good servicepeople, gifted salespeople, and clever marketing personnel are valuable in such times.

SELLING DURING WORRISOME TIMES

The travel industry is highly sensitive to worrisome events. These include natural disasters (e.g., a major earthquake), social turmoil (e.g., rioting), war, governmental factors (a leadership hostile to the Western world takes power) or acts of terrorism (like 9/11/01). Here's what you should keep in mind if events such as these occur (including some ideas from Chapter 7).

- **Consumer behavior is often irrational.** After the 1989 earthquake in Oakland and San Francisco, travel to the region was severely impacted for nearly a year—despite the fact that it was highly unlikely that another earthquake would occur soon. An airplane crash deflects business away from air travel, even though 80,000 takeoffs and landings occur worldwide each day without incident. People often turn to driving vacations, even though automobiles are far more dangerous than air travel.
- **The effect may be specific to industry sectors.** An aircraft hijacking will affect air travel strongly, but concern about motorcoach, rail, ship, and car travel will be much less. (Of course, diminished air travel to departure ports will adversely affect cruising.)
- **Geography plays a big part.** Travelers tend to limit their fears to the specific places where the incident occurred. After the World Trade Center and Pentagon attacks, travel to New York City and Washington, D.C., was especially hard-hit compared to other cities. Consumers' poor geographic knowledge can take over, too. Unrest in the Middle East hurts tourism in, say, Morocco, which is thousands of miles away.
- **Prices can overcome fear.** Low prices have an astonishing ability to erase fear in consumers. During the 1991 Gulf War, people tended to postpone travel—until prices became absurdly low.
- **Repeated events of the same type often reduce fear.** The event becomes a *known* risk and can be addressed more rationally. For example, travelers know that hurricanes occur in the Caribbean from August through October, yet few people will avoid a Caribbean cruise or resort stay during that season. During the 1990s, bombings occurred regularly in the United Kingdom, yet tourism there eventually adapted and even thrived.
- **The travel downturn continues for about six months to a year.** Many experts compare it to grief or mourning, which takes a similar amount of time to work through. Yes, significant industry layoffs can occur throughout the period, but once it's over, *significant hiring and rehiring occur.*

9. **Megachains and consortia will dominate the travel agency market.** Mom-and-pop travel agencies will survive only if they provide exceptional service or target narrow markets.
10. **Some of the predictions you've just read will be wrong.** The 1968 movie *2001: A Space Odyssey* projected our era as one where Pan Am spaceships would fly to orbiting Hiltons. Forecasting the future is a slippery business. Keep this book for ten years, then reread it. You'll be amazed at how many things have changed, some quite unpredictably, and how many things don't ever change.

One prediction however, is certain: If you wish to succeed in travel sales, service or marketing, if you're truly committed to connecting with your travel customers, then you *will* succeed.

Activities **201**

Name: _____ Date: _____

ACTIVITY #1   THE JOB SITUATION

Obtain a copy of a Sunday newspaper (preferably published in a big city) and/or go on the Internet to do a travel job search. What did you find? Answer the questions below:

1. Are they mostly for front-line or executive positions?

2. Do you feel you're qualified for any of them now? Why or why not?

3. Which one intrigued you the most? Why?

4. Is there anything about travel career ads that is any different from other ads? If so, explain.

5. Do you have any observations that weren't covered above?

Name: _____   Date: _____

ACTIVITY #2   YOUR FUTURE IN TRAVEL

Reread the Future of Travel section of this chapter. Select three of the ten predictions and explain how you might develop a travel-related product that would address each. You might also *combine* several predictions. Here's one example:

Since reservationists and travel agents will be on camera, I would create a video training program to show them how to look and communicate best on camera. I would market it to travel schools and professional associations.

Name: _____   Date: _____

ACTIVITY #3 HOW MOTIVATING A MANAGER WOULD YOU BE?

For each of the following statements, rate yourself from 1 to 5 (with 5 being best) and total your score. If you're not a manager, answer according to what you would do if you actually were. At the bottom of the page, you'll see how to interpret your score.

1.	I extend a pleasant greeting to each employee each day.	1	2	3	4	5
2.	I praise and reward employees for good work.	1	2	3	4	5
3.	I offer constructive criticism in private.	1	2	3	4	5
4.	I encourage training and skill development.	1	2	3	4	5
5.	I succeed in resolving employee conflicts.	1	2	3	4	5
6.	I encourage employees to make suggestions.	1	2	3	4	5
7.	I respond quickly to employee requests.	1	2	3	4	5
8.	I keep the staff informed.	1	2	3	4	5
9.	I encourage my staff to accept new challenges.	1	2	3	4	5
10.	I see myself as a team leader.	1	2	3	4	5

Your total score: _____

Scoring:

41–50 points: You're a strong team manager and motivator

31–40 points: You're able to build a strong team

21–30 points: You need to work on your managerial and motivating skills

10–20 points: You're like the boss in "Dilbert"

(Reprinted courtesy of Cruise Lines International Association.)

Glossary

Active cross-selling: When a customer buys an additional product because the seller has suggested it.

Advertising: Promotion that costs something (money or bartered).

Affinity group: A group distinguished by its members' common interest and/or history of shared activities.

Atmosphere: A cue that shapes an overall impression of a business.

Benchmarking: Analyzing what competitors and leading companies in other industries are doing, with the purpose of setting new standards and adopting new strategies for success.

Benefit: How the product affects the buyer.

Brand: A company or product whose name, image and/or reputation are well known to the public.

Brand equity: The value to a company that a brand has to generate awareness and communicate quality.

Business plan: An extended, comprehensive document that a company develops to guide it financially and to help it get bank loans.

Business-to-business selling: Sales situation in which one company sells to another company, not to the public.

Buying motive: A need.

Circle effect: When an entire organization and its customers take on a certain attitude.

Closed-ended question: See Vanguard question.

Cold button: Something that strongly turns off the customer and can defeat the sale.

Coldprospect: A person you approach without him/her expecting your sales effort.

Comment card: A survey you fill out to "grade" different aspects of service.

Commodities: Products that are simple, similar to one other and often bought based on price alone.

Complementary business: When one purchase automatically leads to other, related ones.

Computer Reservation System (CRS): A computer network through which travel products are booked. Also called Global Distribution System.

Consolidator: A company that sells special inventories of products at highly discounted rates.

Consortium: A group of travel agencies that band together to achieve certain advantages, such as buying power, leverage, training, etc.

Consultative research: Using more extensive research to address a client's deeper and more complex travel needs.

Consultative selling: Helping a person make a wise buying decision. A higher level of personal selling that requires deep knowledge, great skill, and a passion to provide the buyer with what he needs and/or wants.

Consumer resource: A resource that the public can access.

Contact overload: A condition caused by dealing with people for hours on end.

Convention and visitors bureau (CVB): Usually a DMO that represents a city, state, or region.

Converting the buyer: Convincing the buyer to buy the product you recommend, rather than what the buyer originally had in mind.

Cooperative (co-op) money: Advertising support from a supplier.

Core sell: The product a customer came to buy initially.

Corporate traveler: A business traveler.

Covert need: A hidden need.

Cross-selling: Offering a buyer the opportunity to purchase allied products that go beyond the obvious core products.

Cross-training: Acquiring skills in several jobs within a company.

Cruise director: The person who coordinates most informational and entertainment activities on the cruise.

Cultural dissonance: Situation in which two societies have different values and behaviors that lead to misinterpretation on one or both sides.

Customer retention program: A program that seeks to address a business's loss of customers.

Database: An organized collection of information—usually computerized—about a company's customers.

Demographics: Easily measurable criteria, such as age, gender, income level, marital status, etc.

Design: How you artistically present your message for maximum effect.

Destination Marketing Organization (DMO): An organization that promotes destinations.

Direct mail: The letters, brochures, postcards, flyers or other, similar items that a company sends through the mail directly to consumers or businesses.

Direct prospecting: Contacting the potential buyer with the intention of making the sales pitch, then and there.

Direct sales model: A sales model in which suppliers sell directly to the public. Also called Retailing.

Discretionary product: A product acquired because the person *chooses* to do so.

Distribution: How you make your product available to consumers.

Escorted tour: A tour in which a tour manager accompanies a group throughout their trip and coordinates their needs.

Exclusive supplier relationship: Arrangement in which the seller offers only one brand in each category of product.

Experiences: Complex products that are different from one another and often bought based on factors much more complicated than price.

Explorer question: A question that uncovers a customer's attitudes, perceptions, feelings, and concerns. Also called Open-ended question.

External contract: An implied agreement on how an employee should treat those outside his/her corporate culture.

External customers: The buying public.

FAQs: Frequently asked questions.

Feature: A fact about a product.

FIT: A trip arranged component by component.

Fixed cost: A cost that doesn't change or hardly changes, no matter what the sales levels are.

Focus group: A group of people, chosen either randomly or in a targeted manner, who, under the guidance of a trained moderator, express their opinions on a service or product.

Frequent-buyer program: See *Loyalty program.*

Front-line employees: Employees who interact directly with the public on a regular basis.

Front-line-to-the-public selling: Sales situation in which the customer and salesperson interact directly.

Global Distribution System (GDS): See *Computer Reservation System.*

Hard adventure travel: Travel that entails extreme physical activities.

Hard sale: A situation in which one company sells a product to another.

Hot button: Something that the client seems especially passionate about.

Impulse buy: A purchase that involves little planning, careful placement and, usually, low cost.

Incentive: A program that uses an awards system to improve work performance.

Independent tour: A package that usually consists of air, hotel, transfers to and from the airport.

Indirect prospecting: Putting yourself in a situation where the opportunity to sell *may* occur.

Indirect sales model: Sales model in which suppliers sell through intermediaries.

Intangible product: A product that can't be seen or touched.

Internal contract: An implied agreement between an employer and employee.

Internal customers: The people within a company whom salespeople work with and must sell ideas to.

Lateral service: When people go beyond their job description to help out service workers in other "departments."

Lead: A person you find out about who may be interested in buying products like yours.

Lifestage: The period of a person's life, especially in the way age determines that person's likes, attitudes and values.

Lifestyle: A way of living that reflects a person's likes, attitudes and values. It often embodies what a person does with his or her leisure time.

Lifestyle question: A question that probes the values that a client holds.

Loss leader: Something that produces little, no, or negative profit, but draws people in, where they're likely to buy other, more profitable things.

Loyalty program: A program that gives customers a reason to keep patronizing a company. Also called Patronage program or Frequent-buyer program.

Macroenvironment: The major, outside forces in a society that affect a business.

Market: All the potential and actual buyers of a product or service.

Marketing: The process of transferring a product from its producer to consumers.

Marketing disconnect: A situation which occurs when a company's marketing team does a great job of giving promotional "spin" to their message, yet fails to communicate and implement that message on a front-line level.

Marketing mix: How product, price, promotion, place, and position come together to create a company's marketing approach.

Marketing plan: A written description of a company's objectives and how these objectives will be achieved.

Mass marketing: Marketing which seeks to attract the greatest number of possible buyers.

Medium: The "channel" you use to communicate your message.

Message: What you're trying to communicate to your customers and to your prospects.

Microenvironment: The forces internal to or close to a company that affect its business.

Moments of truth: Key moments when a customer is most likely to make a decision about a serviceperson and the company he or she represents.

Motivation: An inner urge that prompts a person to act with a sense of purpose. The process of getting people to do what you want them to do.

Mystery shopper: A person hired by a company but unknown to that company's service staff who calls or visits the organization's places of business. The mystery shopper pretends to be a regular customer and observes and later reports on how the employees react to certain predetermined requests.

Net rate: A rate on which the supplier does not pay commission to the seller. The seller's profit comes from marking-up the price.

Niche marketing: Marketing in which a company specializes in very narrowly defined categories of products. Also called Segmentation.

Nonpersonal selling: Sales situation in which the buyer is being motivated not by a person, but by nonpersonal channels, such as advertising.

Open-ended question: See *Explorer question.*

Oral survey: A survey conducted in person or on the phone.

Overt need: An expected need.

Parity: The sameness of products.

Passive cross-selling: When the idea of purchasing something extra occurs without a salesperson initiating it.

Patronage program: See *Loyalty program.*

Pax: Abbreviation for passengers.

Personal packaging: How you and your environment appear to a customer.

Personal selling: Sales in which one person sells to another.

Pied piper: A member of a group, club, or organization who helps promote a tour to the group, usually in return for a free trip.

Preferred relationship: An arrangement in which the seller offers most products for sale, but recommends certain ones over others.

Primary research: Research conducted by a company or association on its own for a specific purpose.

Proactive marketing: Marketing in which a company first decides which buyers it wants and *then* takes steps to reach them.

Product: Anything that's offered to people for purchase and that addresses their needs or wants.

Promotion: The process of making consumers aware of the features, benefits, and availability of your products, with the purpose of getting them to respond to your message and buy.

Promotional mix: How, and in what proportions, promotional tools are blended together.

Promotional rate: A discounted price used to stimulate sales.

Prompt: A cue that appears on a computer screen that reminds the seller to offer other products.

Prospecting: Situation in which a salesperson takes the first step and actively seeks out potential buyers.

Pseudo positioning: A situation in which a company offers a product that's very similar to its competitors, but differentiates itself through superficial tactics.

Psychographics: Harder-to-measure criteria, such as beliefs, values, opinions, desires, and the like.

Publicity: Promotion that costs very little or nothing.

Pull strategy: A strategy in which a company spends most of its advertising funds on consumer promotions to build up demand.

Push strategy: A strategy in which a company promotes its products primarily to intermediaries, who then promote it to consumers.

Recovery: The process of dealing with customer dissatisfaction and complaints.

Relationship marketing: A strategy where a company is dedicated to creating, maintaining, nurturing and enhancing the business it does with customers.

Request for Proposal (RFP):   A company solicitation for bids from suppliers.

Retailing: See *Direct sales model.*

Secondary research: Generic research that others have done—collected perhaps for another purpose.

Segmentation: See *Niche marketing.*

Sell Piece: Anything that helps promote and sell a product or service.

Selling: Offering things for purchase.

Selling up: See *Upselling.*

Service: The way a person and/or company interacts with and treats its customers.

Service gap: An area where performance doesn't match what is expected.

Shells: Preprinted flyers or brochures with photos and graphics, but with large blank spaces for inserting text.

Soft adventure travel: Travel which entails physical activities that reasonably fit people can achieve.

Soft sale: A situation that occurs when no actual product is being sold—the goal is simply to reinforce the seller-buyer relationship and to lay a foundation for future sales.

Specialty retailing: See Niche marketing.

Speculative group: A group departure built around a niche or theme (e.g., a museum tour) and offered to the public.

Stall: Situation in which a customer, despite all that you do, seemingly does not wish to purchase right away.

Tangible product: A product that can be seen and touched.

Target market: A group of buyers who share common characteristics and/or needs that a company decides to serve.

Theming: The process of applying a distinctive, pervasive and entertaining motif to a travel-related experience.

Total Quality Management (TQM):   A principle which states that a company must constantly improve its processes, products, and services to stay competitive.

Tour manager: A person who accompanies, entertains, manages, and narrates multiday tours.

Tourist bureau: Usually a DMO that represents a country. Also called Tourist office.

Tourist office: See *Tourist bureau.*

Trade resource: A resource usually available to travel professionals only.

Transactional research: Simply responding to a customer's logistic and price needs with the particulars of what the salesperson sells.

Transactional selling: Making it possible for someone to buy something; order-taking.

Travel package: Several travel components bundled into one product.

True positioning: A situation in which a company offers a product that's genuinely different from typical products in its category.

Upselling: Offering a buyer the opportunity to purchase a higher, more expensive level of product than the buyer had in mind. Also called Selling up.

Value-added benefit: Something extra you get that you ordinarily wouldn't expect.

Vanguard question: A question that elicits a short, simple, factual answer from the client. Also called Closed-ended question.

Variable cost: A cost that changes according to the sales levels.

VFR travel: Travel to visit friends or relatives.

Wholesaler: A company that sells something to a business for resale.

Within-business selling: Situation in which an employee "sells" an idea to other people within his/her company.

Yield management: A system that measures operations costs, sales revenues, and profit margins so that a company can figure out how much money it's making per customer.

Bibliography

ANDERSON, KRISTIN AND RON ZEMKE. *Delivering Knock Your Socks Off Service*. New York: American Management Association, 1997.

BECKWITH, HARRY. *Selling the Invisible: A Field Guide to Modern Marketing*. New York: Warner Books, 1997.

BLANCHARD, KEN AND SHELDON BOWLES. *Raving Fans: A Revolutionary Approach to Customer Service*. New York: Morrow, William & Co., 1993.

BOSWORTH, MICHAEL. *Solution Selling: Creating Buyers in Difficult Selling Markets*. New York: McGraw-Hill, 1994.

CARLZON, JAN. *Moments of Truth*. New York: Harper, 1989.

CORK, DAVID WITH SUSAN LIGHTSTONE. *The Pig and the Python: How to Prosper from the Aging Baby Boom*. Rocklin, CA: Prima Publishing, 1998.

GITOMER, JEFFREY. *Customer Satisfaction is Worthless, Customer Loyalty is Priceless: How to Make Customers Love You, Keep Them Coming Back and Tell Everyone They Know*. Marietta, GA: Bard Press, 1998.

HEIMAN, STEPHEN E. *The New Strategic Selling*. New York: Warner Books, 1998.

HOUSER, SHELLY M. *Navigate the Net*. Upper Saddle River, NJ: Pearson Education, Inc., 2003.

LEVINSON, JAY CONRAD. *Guerrilla Marketing: Secrets for Making Big Profits from Your Small Business*. Boston: Houghton Mifflin Co., 1998.

MANCINI, MARC. *Conducting Tours* 3e. Albany, NY: Delmar, 2001.

MANCINI, MARC. *Cruising: A Guide to the Cruise Line Industry*. Albany, NY: Delmar, 2000.

MANCINI, MARC. *Selling Destinations* 3e. Albany, NY: Delmar, 1999.

PEOPLES, DAVID A. AND NIGEL HENZELL-THOMAS. *Supercharge your Selling: 60 Tips in 60 Minutes*. New York: Warner Books, 1990.

RIES, AL AND JACK TROUT. *The 22 Immutable Laws of Marketing: Violate Them at Your Own Risk!*. New York: Harper Collins, 1994.

RIES, AL AND LAURA RIES. *The 22 Immutable Laws of Branding: How to Build a Product or Service into a World-Class Brand*. New York: Harper Information, 1998.

SCHIFFMAN, STEPHAN. *The 25 Sales Habits of Highly Successful Salespeople*. Avon, MA: Adams Media, 1994.

STOCKERT, DAVID. *The Idea Machine: 240 Practical & Tactical Marketing Ideas that Really Work*. Seattle: Cruising with Stockert, Inc., 1999.

TREACY, MICHAEL AND FRED WIERSEMA. *The Discipline of Market Leaders*. Cambridge, MA: Perseus Publishing, 1996.

WALTHER, GEORGE R. *Phone Power*. New York: Berkley Books, 1987.

WEINSTEIN, ART. *Market Segmentation: Using Demographics, Psychographics and Other Niche Marketing Techniques to Predict Customer Behavior*. Chicago: Probus Publishing Co., 1994.

WILLINGHAM, RON. *Integrity Selling: How to Succeed in Selling in the Competitive Years Ahead*. New York: Doubleday, 1989.

WUNDERMAN, LESTER. *Being Direct: Making Advertising Pay*. New York: Random House, 1997.

ZEMKE, RON. *The Service Edge: 101 Companies that Profit from Customer Care*. New York: Penguin USA, 1990.

ZIGLAR, ZIG. *Zig Ziglar's Secrets of Closing the Sale*. New York: Berkley Books, 1985.

ZIGLAR, ZIG. *Ziglar on Selling: The Ultimate Handbook for the Complete Sales Professional*. New York: Random House, 1990.

Index